Written and researched by Craig Sams
Published by Alastair Sawday Publishing
Editor: Alastair Sawday
Project editor: Sorrel Everton
Cover design: Caroline King
Overall design concept: Caroline King
Design: Springboard Design Partnership
Original illustrations: David Atkinson
Other illustrations: © 1995 Zedcor, Inc.
Cover image: © ImageState
PR: Jayne Warren
Printing: Compass Press Limited

ISBN 1-901970-32-9

Contents

5 **Foreword** – Derek Cooper
6 **Introduction**
9 **How to use this book**

11 **Pot Noodles and Civilisation** – our world today
13 **Food porn** – chef-obsessed
15 **Eating the View** – a sense of awareness
18 **Slow Food** - taking time
20 **Macrobiotics** – healthy eating – healthy living
23 **Soil and Solutions** – why did we go chemical?
26 **Why Organics?** – why destroy the planet?
29 **Subsidies** – who gains, who loses?
33 **The Digestive System** – chewing it over
36 **Obesity** – dieting can make you fat
38 **Very Fast Food** – and the very slow people it creates
41 **Intensive Agriculture** – how intense can you get?
45 **Deadly Diseases** – the bomb ticks on
48 **The (Not-So?) Green Revolution** – when 'green' isn't good

51 **Food Miles and the Food Chain** – going far?
54 **Supermarkets** – taking control
57 **Tastes Familiar** – fooling your taste buds
60 **The ASA Story** – banning truth about healthy eating
63 **Sweet Nothings** – the truth about sugar
66 **Commodity Markets** – reality distorted
70 **Fair Trade** – how much fairer?
73 **The USA** – if we all ate the way they do
75 **Government** – calling the shots

78 **Join the NFU** – putting your job on the line
81 **Pesticides** – there's no escape
85 **Energy** – it's exhausting
88 **Organophosphates** – the poison hierarchy
91 **Oestrogen** – the feminising hormone
94 **Genetically Modified Food** – but can we eat it?
98 **Fishing for Food** – fishy business
101 **Animal Welfare** – lives at stake

103 **Functional Food** – pharming the food supply
106 **Antibiotics** – the impact on human health
110 **Additives** – hidden and blatant
114 **Wholegrains** – the perfect food
117 **Nutrition and Food Quality** – getting what we need
120 **Brain Food** – think about it
123 **Hydrogenation of Fat** – butter wouldn't melt
126 **Microwaves** – soaking up some rays
129 **Vegetarians** – the barmy army?
132 **Fasting** – take a break
135 **Foreign Climes** – positive approaches to agriculture
138 **Pick 'n' Mix** – a little of what you fancy
140 **Packaging** – a necessary evil?

143 **Brave New World** – guess what's coming to dinner
147 **Grow Your Own** – when mud doesn't matter
149 **Education** – grass-root concerns

152 **Some Conclusions**
154 **References**
160 **Order More Books**

Foreword

Derek Cooper OBE – presenter of BBC Radio 4's *The Food Programme*

Although we have the skill and the technology to put men on the moon and perform complex surgery on the human brain we seem unable to provide the world with wholesome food. Much of the processed junk we are fed is so lacking in nutrition that a parallel industry has sprung up which claims to produce the 'functional' foods we are missing out on. Ironically, the companies marketing them are often major suppliers of highly refined and over-processed food rich in saturated fats, sugar, salt and additives. It is all designed to create the illusion of taste and flavour found in fresh food. We now know that intensive farming may produce cheap food but not necessarily safe food. The growing demand for organic produce is a direct result of 'chemical' farming. People want to know that what they eat is not only safe, but good for their long-term health.

To be intelligent about your diet you need to know how your food is produced. Yet gathering information can be difficult. Food manufacturers spend vast sums of money advertising the virtues of their foods. They are less zealous in drawing attention to the failings. Craig Sams is one of those rare individuals who not only talks in a commonsense way about food but actually produces some pretty good food himself. His company, Whole Earth, has played a major role in promoting the idea that processed food can be good food. When I first met him I was impressed by this maverick views. Here was an American who was making baked beans in London and exporting them to the US.

The Little Food Book is a global guide. It's about our use and misuse of the land and the seas. It addresses the major issues behind the current food debate and it presents an alternative view, which could lead to better health and a better life for the whole world.

Introduction

It was hepatitis, ironically, that gave me my first awareness of the importance of food to health. In 1965, travelling from India to Afghanistan, I developed hepatitis and was left at a low ebb. After following a macrobiotic diet, I recovered completely. In February 1966 I made a trip to New York to visit the macrobiotic bookshop on 5th Avenue. When I took some books to the till a rather morose woman told me that I couldn't buy them. They were awaiting a decision from the FBI before they could sell books again! At the instigation of the American Medical Association, the FBI had entered the shop and taken away books to see if they broke the law. They did. The books suggested that cancer could be prevented – even cured – by healthy eating. These were sufficiently serious offences to justify the removal of the books. They were subsequently burned. The bookshop closed soon after and many shocked members of the small New York macrobiotic community moved to Chico, a town in northern California.

Such vehement reactions to macrobiotics were an extended attack that implied quasi-terrorist attributes to people who believed that 'you are what you eat'. It was a depressing moment, especially for anyone who had experienced the happiness that comes from vigorous good health based on a balanced diet of wholesome natural foods. Against the background of the Vietnam War, eating a macrobiotic diet became a political statement – one that was adopted by large numbers of my generation. The same evening as my visit to the bookshop, I also visited the Paradox, a macrobiotic restaurant in the East Village, and it was then I decided to change the plans for my life. I decided to open a macrobiotic restaurant in London, which I did in 1967.

As with so many ideas of the 1960s, macrobiotics, natural foods, healthy eating and organic living are no longer considered 'lunatic fringe'. Today the Harvard School of Public Health even suggests macrobiotics to avoid increasing obesity and diet-related disease. That little group of macrobiotics who moved to Chico set up a food company called Chico-San to distribute brown rice and similar foods. In 1998 Heinz bought it to give them entry into the organic food market in the USA. The expenditure on complementary and alternative healthcare in the US now exceeds spending on surgery and pharmaceuticals. Many doctors now have qualifications in nutrition, homeopathy and other therapies. They need them to be able to offer their patients a more holistic and preventative approach to health.

Since adopting a macrobiotic diet I have not needed a doctor and have taken no prescription drug. I have been ill at times but have learned to respect the importance of a healthy digestive system. My children have grown up with stronger constitutions and straighter teeth than I have. To me they are living proof that a diet that includes minimal meat and dairy products, and is weighted strongly towards whole grains and vegetables, can support health and strength. My grandchildren's physical robustness and balanced dispositions indicate that, notwithstanding Darwin, acquired characteristics can be inherited. We have the power to evolve in whatever direction we choose and what we eat can exercise a profound influence on us at the chromosomal level. We know that bad nutrition can lead to physical degeneration and that this can be inherited – the children of diabetics are more likely to develop diabetes. It follows that the children of healthy parents will be less likely to develop chronic illness.

The political attacks on macrobiotics taught me to regard the opinions of experts and government officials with a healthy scepticism. Mandy Rice-Davies' famous maxim, 'He would say that, wouldn't he?', rings in my ears whenever I read that researchers and scientists have proved that white bread is better for you than wholemeal, that cancer is caused by a virus, that once we map the human genome we can cure all diseases, that without sugar we will lack energy and that meat is the best protein. Food, and its influence on physical and mental well-being, has been at the centre of my business career and my personal life. Sometimes I may have been a bit fanatical. But 'fanum' means 'temple' and my body is my temple. I have looked extensively within and come to understand, through intuition, experience and study of the observations of others, how it works and how to keep it working well. I find it hard to accept science when it runs counter to my intuition and experience. But science, too, is beginning to take a more holistic view.

The world's diet is getting worse and better simultaneously. Every day another four MacDonald's restaurants open somewhere in the world – harbingers of a diet and lifestyle that leads inexorably to obesity. The diseases that arise from obesity and digestive malfunction are increasing as a modern, fast food diet displaces traditional ways of eating around the world. Yet, the numbers who go to bed hungry are still near one sixth of the world's population.

Nonetheless, every day more people choose to step off the junk food treadmill and enjoy a form of personal freedom. When they do so, the infrastructure that provides organic, natural and wholesome food expands a little bit more. Despite government policy that still bends to powerful pharmaceutical, medical and chemical interests, a new consensus about how and what we should eat, what is and isn't safe, is emerging. It is growing in the ever-crucial marketplace, and I am filled with optimism.

This little book will, I hope, contribute to that emerging consensus. It tackles key issues like nutrition, the politics of food and the mainsprings of health. If we all ate with an awareness of the importance of our food choices, there would be more health and justice on this crowded planet. With justice comes peace – the ultimate goal of civilisation.

Craig Sams - author

This is a book with a fascinating range, but the dominant message is: pay attention to what you eat. Much of it harms you and the environment, and neither the Government nor the food industry is on your side. This remarkable book will encourage you to take back responsibility for your own nutritional health. In the process you will not only have fun but you will be doing your bit for the planet.

Alastair Sawday - publisher

How to use this book

Dip in and out if you wish; take a subject at a time. Each chapter is short and to the point – however vast the subject – and aims to provoke you, both emotionally and intellectually. Do read further; the book symbol at the end of some chapters refers you to books and websites that go more deeply into the subjects, though the views expressed here don't necessarily represent the views of those books.

Better still, try reading it all at one or two sittings; the ideas, held together in your memory, will form a powerful whole. For that is the strength of this book: we cannot consider 'food' as an isolated issue. It is linked to far greater global problems. The book is roughly divided into five sections: general issues; food and big business; food and farming; food and nutrition, and thoughts to ponder. The range of issues is broad but they are all far too important not to be considered, as you will see.

"When the sun rises, I go to work
When the sun goes down, I take my rest
I dig the well from which I drink
I farm the soil that yields my food,
I share creation, Kings can do no more."

Anonymous (Chinese, 2500BC)

Pot Noodles and Civilisation

our world today

The rise in the total level of wealth and education in the world has been dramatic throughout the 20th century – despite two world wars,. More people have more money and more valuable property than ever before. Secondary education is almost universal, university education widespread. Growing inequalities may mar the picture, but the level of wealth enjoyed by the large numbers of 'haves' greatly exceeds anything in the past. Even many 'have-nots' may still have proper sanitation and televisions and can choose to afford highly taxed products like alcohol and cigarettes.

This overall wealth has brought huge benefits. The air we breathe is much cleaner than it was when coal was routinely burned by industry and in the home and when lead in fuel was standard. The food we eat is free of many of the worst additives and adulterants that were once permitted. The water we drink conforms to new, more rigorous standards. Rivers are cleaner. Emphasis on safety in the workplace, in cars and in airplanes makes work and travel less likely to cause death or disability. The value society places on human life encourages us, as our individual and collective net worth increases, to improve our living conditions and invest to minimise the risk of threats to life.

So what on earth has gone wrong with our food? Food-related deaths exceed by many times deaths from car accidents and the rate is escalating. Diabetes, heart disease, obesity and cancer all point to a depressingly awful quality of life for increasing numbers of young people as they carry these (often) food-related diseases into adulthood. When we look at the range of what we eat, there has been an explosion of variety and sophistication with 'world fusion' cuisine as an expected norm. Yet there has been a parallel surge in nutritionally poor, unsafe food.

Confectionery was once a luxury and occasional treat. Now chocolate bars and flapjacks, concoctions of sugar, hydrogenated fat and flavourings, replace meals. Pot noodles, refined flour packed with flavourings and artificial flavour enhancers, provide a plastic wrapped hot snack for those whose only cooking skill lies in switching on a kettle or a microwave. Hamburgers, hot dogs, pizzas and other fast foods drive down the quality of farming and processing practice. Soft drinks replace other drinks, leading to large increases in sugar intake. The result is a dietary disaster area. Never have so many eaten so much fat and sugar.

How is it that a civilisation that has brought so much progress in so many areas of human aspiration and idealism has let us down so badly in our most important activity – eating – and its equally important goal – health? It is easy to blame big business and agricultural pressure groups. But perhaps the real blame lies with us, with the casual, even careless approach we apply to how we grow and choose our food.

People who get a grip on their diet not only enjoy their food much more; they enjoy better health, happiness and longevity. It is terribly unfair that innocent children, born into modern, prosperous democratic societies – and too young to know any better – should be trapped in a vicious cycle of junk food addiction that will shorten their lives and make them forever dependent. How can we get it together to have food and diet worthy of the achievements of our civilisation?

The human species is facing evolutionary change. Two hundred years ago the average height of a European shot up by 30 cm. Today the change is not upwards but outwards. In 1980, the average man weighed 73.7 kg and a woman 62.2 kg By 2000, that had increased to 81.6 kg and 68.8 kg respectively.

Food Porn

chef-obsessed

Is gourmet cooking the new rock 'n' roll – or just an above-the-navel branch of pornography?

Television offers more than 40 hours of food programming a week, and over the last five years the number of magazines about food and cooking doubled, their circulation tripled and readership quadrupled. Videos are set so that avid fans don't miss Delia's latest tricks with an egg or Nigella whipping some cream.

Fans of pornography argue that revelling in visual images of sex is a lot safer than all that messy business involving dating, seduction and dealing with bodily fluids issues. For the food porn fan, how much healthier to let the eyes do the eating and avoid all that messy business with shopping, cooking and dealing with bodily fat issues. Besides, the real thing is never presented with such panache, perfect lighting, artistic arrangements, voyeuristic camera angles and sparkling voiceovers. As every food stylist knows, Vaseline plays a crucially important role, giving a glistening sheen to that lovingly photographed, glazed, maple-balsamic turkey breast.

It all started in 1960 with Elizabeth David. Her groundbreaking book *French Provincial Cooking* offered something new and exciting to Brits emerging from the shadow of rationing. In her introduction she advocated *faites simple* – 'keep it simple'. But her three-page recipe for cassoulet (mastery of which was the *sine qua non* for marrying well in the 60s) was an Everest of complexity to a generation reared on egg and chips. She laid down the new ground rules for food, saying it should be "civilised without being over-civilised. That is to say, it has natural taste, smell, texture and much character. Often it looks beautiful, too. What it amounts to is that it is the rational, right and proper food for human beings to eat."

This heralded a total break from the post war concern with simply getting enough food, and from the stuffiness of haute cuisine. It struck a chord in the nation's stomach.

In 1983 Alastair Little's reign at 192, the hip Notting Hill eaterie, trained and unleashed on the world the generation of British chefs who were hailed from Sydney to the Upper West Side as the samurai of the new, sexy cuisine. The young superchefs indulged their quirky personalities, throwing tantrums in the kitchen as regularly as rock stars would throw televisions out of hotel windows. To be a chef on TV it still helps to have a restaurant with a smart clientèle and a cookbook to go with the series. Cookbooks top the non-fiction best-seller lists all the year round.

If cooking is the new rock 'n' roll then its Johnny Rotten must surely be Anthony Bourdain, whose confessional *Kitchen Confidential* is a warts-and-all description of drug-crazed kitchen antics that will give extra edge to those contemplating a fusion food menu.

When it comes to cooking at home, what with all those food magazines, cookbooks and TV shows to get through, a phone call to the takeaway saves time and hassle. The convenience food market grew by 400 per cent in the 1990s. Inevitably perhaps, the more we watch other people cook, the less we do it ourselves. When we do cook, we rarely do so 'from scratch', relying on prepared ingredients to ensure that everything goes to recipe once we get the apron on.

But behind it all is a growing appreciation that food is fun as well as fuel, that you can eat well and be well, that health and happiness are not mutually exclusive at the dinner table. Gastro-porn does indeed signal the emergence of a new food culture.

Desirable urban apartments are now built with tiny, if no, kitchens. They offer little more than areas for a fridge, microwave and kettle.

Kitchen Confidential
Anthony Bourdain
Bloomsbury 2001
ISBN 0 747 55355 6

Eating the View

a sense of awareness

You don't have to be an artist to appreciate beautiful countryside. Most of us are repelled by the sight of featureless expanses of barley and fields stripped of hedgerows, let alone covered by ugly buildings housing intensively reared farm animals.

In October 2001 Sandra Pepys, President of The British Society of Landscape Painters, organised an exhibition of landscape art at the Mall Galleries in London. All the artists represented agreed to give one third of their income from the show to The Council for the Protection of Rural England and the Soil Association, Britain's leading organic organisation. Their offer acknowledged that the countryside they chose to paint often turned out to be under organic cultivation. A simple example of how individual actions count as a vote for both the kind of countryside consumers enjoy, and the food production practices they prefer. By literally 'eating the view' – the 'man in the street' can support rural communities and initiatives.

Money circulates and the longer it can stay in a local area the more value it has. It is estimated that £10 spent in a supermarket on imported processed foods quickly finds its way out of the community and even out of the country. However, £10 spent on locally produced food has the economic impact of £28, as it changes hands several times before

finding its way into the mainstream. Local producers earn a higher margin, saving on transport costs and benefiting from the added value of any processing they do themselves. This supports the rural economy, without which much of the countryside would be little other than barren expanses of subsidised cereals.

On 30 March 2000, the British Prime Minister called on the Countryside Agency, a government body, to: "assist consumers in understanding the connections between the food they buy and the countryside they value, and to work with others to develop projects to achieve this aim".

The Countryside Agency's job is to look after the countryside, socially, economically and environmentally. Among other organisations helping them to achieve this is the Soil Association, whose 'Local Food Links' programme, established in 1994, has developed 'box schemes' and farmers' markets.

Box schemes involve consumers buying a regular supply of seasonal vegetables from a local producer, who then enjoys financial security. Farmers' markets put the customer in touch with the person who grew and harvested the food – perhaps that very morning.

Sadly, many regional foods have lost their 'branding'. 'Cheddar' cheeses from Wisconsin, Hamburg or Manchester are rubbery alternatives to the real thing. We need to establish clear regional identities for foods to protect the high quality that comes with 'regionality'. And indeed, there is growing public interest in the countryside, food safety and production methods, and a recognition that buying local products helps local communities. What's more most farmers would rather diversify than dance to the tune of remote bureaucrats in Brussels.

So, alternative retailing systems are flourishing, after a period when village stores have been struggling – or closing. Supermarkets, in their turn, are trying to meet the new demand for foods that have character and regional or local identity. The dead hand of centralised and intensive agriculture has held sway over the countryside for too many decades. Government, at last, recognises that it is much easier to integrate its environmental, social and economic goals if it encourages 'eat the view' practices.

The new 'green consumerism' links wholesome food, beautiful countryside and sustainable agriculture. Entrepreneurialism may not come easily to farmers, but a new generation can thrive on such challenges. The average age of British farmers is 59, a sure sign of a declining industry. 'Eating the view' can transform the countryside and the prospects of those who live in it while bringing fresh, wholesome and sustainably produced food to consumers. With lower food miles, less packaging and higher standards of animal welfare, 'eating the view' is a win-win-win opportunity and one that will encourage the move towards organic standards of production.

Bringing the Food Economy Home
Norberg-Hodge, Merrifield, Gorelick
Zed Books 2000
ISBN 1 842 77232 5

Slow Food

taking time

Slow is beautiful

The 'Slow Food' movement started in Bra, a small town in the Piedmont region of Italy, at the foot of the Alps. It was prompted by the opening of a McDonald's restaurant in Rome in 1986 and adopted the slogan: **"A firm defense of quiet material pleasure is the only way to oppose the universal folly of fast life".**

Founded by Carlo Petrini, the Slow Food movement, with the snail as its symbol, focused initially on food and wine and produced a best-selling guide to Italian gastronomical treats.

But Petrini had a still greater vision – eco-gastronomy. "I want Slow Food not to be merely a **gastronomical organisation** but [one that] deals with problems of the environment and world hunger without renouncing the right to pleasure," he said.

Perhaps as a reaction to its fast food culture, the US has seen rapid Slow Food growth. "The United States is natural Slow Food territory," says Petrini. "You have a huge move toward organic food and ... microbreweries. Up until 10 or 20 years ago, you had two large companies [Busch and Miller] that dominated the beer market. Now you have 1,600 microbreweries."

Slow Food even has an office in Brussels. Here, they successfully protect many Italian producers from the complex administrative requirements that are impossible for small producers, whose time is spent producing high-quality food, to comply with. When they set out to protect the Piedmontese cow, whose numbers were diminishing, Slow Food helped livestock producers to adopt organic and additive-free methods to produce a higher quality, lower fat beef. Market success came slowly, until BSE was discovered in Italian beef. Piedmontese beef quickly became every Italian's first choice.

Slow Food now has 65,000 members in 50 countries organised in 560 'convivia'. In the US alone there are over 62 chapters. Its *Salone del Gusto* is Italy's most popular food fair and draws international attention. Small food producers, 'natural stewards of biodiversity', have discovered that shared ethical values can create global opportunities. Typical of these is Veli Galas, a Turkish beekeeper. He won the Slow Food Award for a honey made in the trunks of trees in a forest near the Black Sea.

The Slow Food Movement has led to Slow Cities, where the quality of food is the foundation for a cultural, environmental and 'eco-gastronomic' approach to urban life. Over 30 Italian towns are now members. Though none has yet earned the coveted 'cittaslow' snail logo, it is hoped that cities and towns worldwide will move toward attaining 'Slow City' status and set an example of how urban living can satisfy 'neo-humanist' aspirations. Many participating towns have already seen economic growth. The US Newsweek magazine even suggested that Slow Food and Cittaslow were a unique, Italian response to globalisation.

Key requirements to become a Slow City include:
- Encouraging good food with farmers' markets, traditional cuisine, organic agriculture, and no genetically modified products.
- Prohibiting car alarms, TV aerials, advertising billboards and neon signs.
- Ecological transport with cycle paths, expanded pedestrian areas, and limits on cars.
- Tree planting, recycling and new parks.
- Urging businesses, schools, and government offices to adjust hours to enable people to enjoy a slow midday meal with family and friends.

Slow Food sees children as the Slow Foodies of the future and seeks to educate them in the taste of food and in how it is produced. They even produce a book teaching kids about flavour and its appreciation through 'aware' tasting.

Slowfoodplanet Directory
www.slowfood.com

Macrobiotics

healthy eating – healthy living

Definition:
1. 'great life', in both length and quality;
2. the seeker after health and longevity.

Macrobiotics was the only wholefood/healthy eating message of the 1960s and 70s, inspiring the natural foods and organic movement. The first natural food stores that appeared in the 70s in the US and Europe stuck to macrobiotic principles, selling grains and pulses and organic vegetables and avoiding processed foods, especially any containing sugar.

Macrobiotic medicine mirrors elements of traditional Japanese folk medicine but puts primary emphasis on diet. *Zen Macrobiotics*, by George Ohsawa was the original guide to macrobiotic living. In it he describes positive health. "Health is not just the absence of disease but is defined in positive terms as: **No fatigue, good appetite, deep and good sleep, good memory, good humour, clarity of thinking and doing and, most importantly, gratitude.** The four-part way to achieve this is set out as: Natural food, no medicine, no surgery, no inactivity. "

Macrobiotic directions for a natural food diet are:
- No industrialised food and drink such as sugar, soft drinks, dyed food, canned or bottled food
- Wholegrains and vegetables as the core of the diet with animal products eaten in smaller amounts or not at all. When Ohsawa wrote there was no organic meat industry so he proposed occasional game and fish
- Food should be produced without chemical fertilisers and pesticides, i.e organic food
- Avoid food that comes from a long distance
- Choose foods in season – eating in season harmonises with the body's natural seasonal changes. (It also ensure freshness and avoids preservatives.)

- Avoid nightshades: aubergine, potato, tomato – they contain toxic solanine alkaloids
- No chemical seasonings (i.e. msg), colouring or preservatives
- No coffee, although tea is allowed
- Yeasted foods kept to a minimum – natural leaven preferred
- Chew every mouthful 50 times or more.
- Low liquid intake – Ohsawa argued that kidney function did not need large amounts of water.

Some of these may seem excessive, but it was macrobiotics that introduced us to the 'brown rice and lentils' of the alternative lifestyle. A diet high in wholegrains, pulses and vegetables was certainly cheaper than a diet based on processed foods, animal products and imported luxuries, but it was its health benefits that spurred devotees on.

The Taoist principle of complementary opposites, Yin and Yang, underpins macrobiotic theory. Some foods are more yang, others more yin. A food's characteristics, when consumed, translates into a similar yin-yang balance in the consumer. In this way, if one is overexcited and energetic (excess yang) one can eat more bland yin foods to reach a less stressed state – cabbage, carrots, milk, pears and potatoes. If one is tired and dreamy (excess yin) one can energise and focus by choosing more rich and hot yang foods – beef, chicken, eggs, peanuts, peppers and onions. Success in macrobiotics comes when you find a healthy equilibrium and then instinctively choose the foods that maintain it.

The concept of 'biological transmutation' infuses macrobiotics, the idea that the digestive system can create nutrients that are not already in the food you eat. It argues that if you eat the right foods, a healthy body will extract the balance of nutrients that it needs, manufacturing them if necessary in the gut flora or by other processes.

Many macrobiotic-dieters, however, stuck too rigidly to the rules, with poor results. Ohsawa advised against such rigidity, arguing that the healthy constitution achieved through macrobiotics confers the ability to relax sometimes the rules with no ill effect.

Good health is one aspect of macrobiotic living. On a broader level, macrobiotics also aspires to a central role in bringing about social evolution

and global stability. Ohsawa even saw world peace as the eventual successful outcome of the universal practice of macrobiotics.

The 'win-win' equation runs: **healthy food = healthy people = healthy societies = peace.** Ohsawa died in 1966, just a few months before the 'Peace Olympics' which he had planned. One of his colleagues, Michio Kushi, went on to found 'East-West' macrobiotic study centres around the world and the movement is still active and growing. The core ideas of macrobiotics had also entered the mainstream. Back in 1966 Dr. Fredrick Stare, the eminent Harvard nutritionist, wrote in Reader's Digest: "Macrobiotics is the diet that's killing our kids", so alarmed was he at its departure from convention. Today the Harvard School of Public Health cites macrobiotics as an example of the kind of diet that Americans should adopt to avoid diet-related health disease and getting fat.

Ohsawa urged macrobiotic-followers to read *Erewhon*, the novel by Samuel Butler, describing a Utopia in which sick people are thrown in prisons and criminals treated in hospitals. In 1974 a Pennsylvania prison initiated a programme of macrobiotic food for prisoners. Rates of violence fell, as did the number of re-offences.

Macrobiotics for Beginners
Jo Sandifer, Bob Lloyd
Piatkus 2000
ISBN 0 749 92119 6

Soil and Solutions

why did we go chemical?

Way back in 1836, with the science of chemistry in its infancy, one food technologist, Baron Justus von Liebig, took a look at what made plants grow and what made food taste good. He worked out that the key elements in soil that nourished plants were nitrogen, phosphorus and potassium and decided to 'improve' soil by synthesising these ingredients himself. This was the start of 'modern' farming.

His ideas didn't catch on, the chemicals cost money and, although in the short term crop yields improved, farmers found that they needed more and more chemicals in order to maintain yields. The economics simply didn't work. By 1863, when Liebig was 65 years old, he was disillusioned with his attempts to help farming and he wrote: "I have sinned against the Creator and, justly, I have been punished. I wanted to improve His work because, in my blindness, I believed that a link in the astonishing chain of laws that govern and constantly renew life on the surface of the Earth had been forgotten. It seemed to me that weak and insignificant man had to redress this oversight".

Chemicals, nonetheless, continued to play a part in agriculture – as a short-term fix to build up soil fertility and as part of the curriculum at agricultural colleges. Meanwhile, the American prairies, a vast, unexploited reservoir of fertility, were opened up to farming, and European agriculture had to struggle against cheap imports of American wheat and beef.

However, by the 1930s the soil fertility of the American Midwest was so exhausted that the Dust Bowl became a devastating reality. The humus-exhausted topsoil, no longer held together by organic matter, simply blew away. This event shocked farmers around the world and the organic movement was born.

A study of Chinese, Korean and Japanese agriculture, *Farmers of Forty Centuries*, by F. H. King (1911) showed how farmers had increased the fertility of their farmland by returning organic matter to the soil. Around the same time Sir Albert Howard, in India to teach modern agricultural methods, soon realised that he had more to learn than to teach. He was the father of modern composting, bringing the 'Indore Process' back to Britain, where it was enthusiastically adopted by many British farmers. Among these was Lady Eve Balfour who used it at her farm in Haughley, Essex. She went on to found the Soil Association, the founding organisation of the global organic movement, in 1946. The term 'organic' came to describe what was previously known as 'permanent farming' i.e. **farming that could be sustained forever without exhausting the land.**

The Second World War showed the need for agricultural self-sufficiency. It also led to tremendous growth in the production of nitrogen-based explosives and toxic organophosphorous chemicals which were developed as potential nerve gas weaponry. ICI (Imperial Chemical Industries) was a major supplier of these chemicals only to find itself with huge overcapacity at the end of the war. As debates raged about the future direction of agriculture, ICI lobbied heavily for the wider use of agrichemicals. It needed to divert its production capacity from a war on the Axis powers to a war on Nature, using nitrates and pesticides as the primary weapons. The Soil Association proposed a continuation of wartime quasi-organic methods and argued that healthy soils were needed to produce healthy plants and animals if humans themselves were to enjoy good health. Farmers were cautious about adopting agrichemicals as they knew only too well the dangers of exhausting fertility and becoming dependent on artificial fertilisers.

The Agriculture Act of 1947, however, paid out generous subsidies on every bag of fertiliser, thus stimulating a major move towards the use of chemical aids. While increased yields became the norm, soil structure, fertility and health declined and plants became more prone to insect and fungal attack. Weeds also grew rapidly when fertilisers were applied, so herbicide use boomed. All these chemicals inevitably damaged the environment.

But by now farmers, or at least their land, were addicted to chemicals. When in 1974 Britain joined the EEC (and the Common Agricultural Policy), subsidies on fertilisers were dropped. Instead the crops themselves were subsidised by guaranteed prices. This led to overproduction and surpluses, which were dumped on developing countries, damaging the livelihoods of small farmers, many of whom were driven out of business and forced to migrate to urban centres. Here 'aid', in the form of cheap or free bread and powdered milk, kept them alive, while they sought work as cheap labour or migrated to Europe or North America to look for work.

The organic movement looked stymied. While Governments subsidised overproduction, farmers would use artificial fertilisers in preference to natural methods. Consider, for example that there have never been subsidies for a field of clover, even though it increases the nitrogen and the humus content of the soil. But a core of organic farmers soldiered on, committed to doing right by the land and by nature. By the 1960s a market for their products was emerging among consumers who did not want pesticide residues in their food or to see the countryside ruined.

That market continues to grow today.

- In 1974 the Soil Association produced the world's first written standards that defined exactly what food production qualified as organic.

- The organic market was worth a mere £3 million in 1974 but worth over £1 billion in the UK by 2001.

- Globally the market for organic food now exceeds £20 billion, with Germany and the United States, the countries where agrochemicals had once been most enthusiastically adopted, showing the fastest growth.

The Organic Tradition
Philip Conford (Ed)
Green Books 1988
ISBN 1 870098 09 9

Why Organics?

why destroy the planet?

Why do so many producers, consumers and policymakers see 'organics' as a desirable alternative to conventional farming? Well, the arguments for organics are powerful: food safety and quality, sustainability, environment, employment, rural economy and animal welfare.

Food Safety and Quality

Most organic consumers seek, above all, to avoid pesticides. The traceability required for all certified organic food ensures strict standards for growing and processing. Excluded are pesticides, processing chemicals, genetically modified organisms (GMOs), hydrogenated fats, phosphoric acid, artificial colourings, preservatives, artificial sweeteners and flavour enhancers, hormones and antibiotics. Not everyone cares about all these things, but only organic food offers a comprehensive guarantee of their absence – backed up by an international inspection and certification system. Although organic rules allow white sugar, white flour, alcohol (there's even organic rum) and other foods that are not really 'healthy', organic food appeals to the health-conscious (those who eat more vegetables, fruit and fibre and less fat and sugar).

In April 2001, The Worthington Study reviewed 41 other studies carried out on crops grown using organic matter or inorganic fertilisers. In all cases the organic crops had higher levels of Vitamin C (27 per cent more), magnesium (29 per cent), iron (21 per cent) and phosphorus (14 per cent).

Sustainability

Organic farming began with concerns about the loss of topsoil, disappearing forests and the risk that we could run out of land to feed ourselves. Fossil fuels and carbon output are extra concerns.

To rebuild topsoil, organic farmers plant green manures, make compost and undersow crops with clover to increase organic matter (humus) in soil. The result is better water retention and soil fertility. Conventional agriculture loses arable land every year. One cause is salination: chemical fertilisers destroy humus so that frequent irrigation is needed, water retention is minimal and salts build up. This can't be sustained. Building humus also captures and stores carbon, thus reducing global warming. Organic farmers who plough only occasionally and use green manures can accumulate up to one tonne of carbon per hectare per year. Organic farming also uses less fossil fuel, preferring human labour to heavy machinery. Fertilisers and pesticides are made from fossil fuels, too; organic farmers use less of them.

The arithmetic of farming can appear ludicrous: it takes 12 calories of fossil fuels to produce one calorie of food grain in industrial agriculture. Organic farming uses five calories. Organic arable production can be 35 per cent more energy efficient, and organic dairy production 74 per cent more efficient than non-organic production. Worldwide, farmers now use 10 times more fertiliser and spend 17 times more on pesticides as in 1950. The share of the harvest lost to pests, however, is unchanged.

The Environment

Organic farms generally support higher levels of wildlife. Forty per cent more birds were found in a three-year UK study of 44 farms, twice as many butterflies and five times as many wild arable plants.

Further, no nitrate fertiliser is used on organic farms and there are limits on manure use; so nitrate pollution of water is low. Excess nitrate runoff causes algae growth that de-oxygenates water, killing fish and aquatic plants.

Employment

The use of pesticides, herbicides, chemical fertilisers, intensive animal rearing systems and the creation of bigger fields mean fewer workers. So, rural employment declines and poverty among farmers increases. Of the 1.2 billion people who earn less than one dollar a day, 800 million live in rural areas. In the US in 1950 half of the money spent on food found its way to the farmer. The figure today is just seven per cent. The difference goes to processors, chemical companies, machinery suppliers and agribusiness cartels. Research on 200 organic projects in the developing world showed that conventional yields could increase by 93 per cent – and more. Employment and soil fertility also increase.

Rural Economy

As Government policies force farm labourers off the land, the rural economy declines. Money earned and spent locally circulates several times and supports rural communities. A farmer who buys in chemicals and machinery, and ships out products, has little effect on the local economy. Many Midwestern states in the US are now suffering rural de-population and some farm families are now dependent on food donations.

Animal Welfare

Organic standards for animal care are strict. In 2002 Compassion in World Farming compared the standards for organic farms against 15 criteria for animal welfare. Organic farming achieved

between 11 and 14 out of 15 for five different livestock groups. Conventional systems scored between four and seven. Much of the growth in the sale of organics has come from vegetarians, many of whom have converted to eating organic meat because they approve of the animal welfare standards.

People often choose organic food for specific reasons – avoidance of a particular pesticide such as lindane or horror at the cruelties inflicted on battery hens. However, as the whole range of issues is further understood, the commitment to eating organically deepens.

About 2,000 million hectares of soil have been degraded through human activities – that's 15% of the Earth's land area, an area larger than the US and Mexico combined.

Organic Farming, Food Quality
and Human Health
Soil Association
ISBN 0 905200 80 2

Subsidies

who gains, who loses?

Subsidies keep foods such as hamburgers and hydrogenated fat cheap and thus encourage obesity among overfed Westerners. But their real victims are smaller family farms and the global economy. Real hardship and poverty are caused, worldwide, by the subsidy system of the US and EU. Rich countries' subsidies to their own farmers amount to seven times their annual foreign aid of $50 billion. Along with protectionist tariff barriers they prevent those poor countries' farmers from selling their products to the rich world.

So how do subsidies cause poverty?

1. Cheap exports of subsidised surplus food undermine local agricultural economies; farmers cannot compete with subsidised grain.

2. World prices for all food are kept artificially low by subsidies. This is the main cause of poverty among the billion farmers worldwide who earn less than $1 per day. Although cheap food prices help those on low incomes, the urban poor should not be used as an excuse for keeping the rural poor in poverty. It is rural poverty that fuels the exodus to the urban slums. The foundation of developing country economies is agriculture, usually 50-80 per cent of gross national product (GNP) compared to one per cent of US or UK GNP. If farmers do well, the whole economy thrives. The more farmers earn, the more they spend on material goods and, crucially, the more they spend on educating their kids giving them the opportunity of better jobs with better wages.

3. Subsidies also drive small farmers in the US and EU countries out of business. They support large farms that practise environmentally damaging monoculture.

Cheap Exports

Farm policy in the US and EU involves buying the farmers' surpluses and storing them. These are then dumped as 'aid' or sold cheap to developing countries. Some surpluses are converted into meat and dairy products that are then exported or given away – a convenient disposal route.

In Mexico, where subsidised American maize is imported under the North American Free Trade Agreement (NAFTA), 15 million people will lose their livelihoods. Without US subsidies Mexican farmers could export maize  to the US. In the dry Sahel countries of Africa, small farmers cannot compete with EU dumping of surplus subsidised cereals and so move to the cities in search of work. The land is left to pastoral nomads whose animals graze away what little vegetation there is, increasing desertification.

World Food Price Distortion

It is the Chicago Board of Trade that sets low prices for agricultural commodities: pork bellies, beef, corn, soybeans, wheat and soybean oil. These prices then become the yardstick for world pricing. It might be called a 'market', but prices are more the result of Government subsidy policy than of market laws of supply and demand. All this influence – and the US has only eight per cent of the world's arable land!

The average American farm now earns half its income from government subsidies, but the level of subsidy to corn and soybean farmers is higher still – nearly 100 per cent. Without subsidies prices would have to double and the income of all the world's food producers would increase dramatically.

EXAMPLE

A farmer in Kenya grows maize at a cost of 4.5 cents per pound, which is more than the US 'market' price of 3.5 cents per pound. But the true cost of production to an American farmer is 6 cents per pound. In this topsy-turvy world, the more efficient Kenyan farmer can't compete with less efficient American farmers who have the mighty American taxpayer subsidising their farm-gate price.

If the Chicago price was unsubsidised, the Kenyan farmer could compete and become more profitable. He would be able to pay for healthcare, education and manufactured goods – all to the benefit and future stability of Kenya. Instead, if the Kenyan farmer tries to sell for five cents per pound, in an attempt to make a profit, grain traders will import the cheaper American corn (cheaper even with freight costs).

Emigration, war and refugees are the result of agricultural communities going bankrupt. The lucky ones get a job in Europe or the USA, often illegally and in exploitative conditions; quite often – ironically – in agriculture. They then send their earnings home, to support their families who have stayed behind on the land. It is a wasteful and inefficient way of allocating the world's human and agricultural resources.

Harm to American and European small farmers
Family farmers, including organic farmers, receive lower levels of subsidy. Without subsidies big farmers would profit less from planting prairies of rape and barley or intensifying animal production. Small-scale farming would stage a comeback. Food prices might go up a little, but probably no more than the £20 per week per household that the Common Agricultural Policy

costs. The CAP spends half its annual budget on subsidies to farmers, a quarter on storage and warehousing costs and a quarter on administration costs and fraud control. A child could see the waste in this.

So who gains from subsidies?
• Big farming corporations do. The subsidy system encourages 'monoculture', mainly of feed crops. The large, heavily mechanised agribusinesses, the biggest users of chemical fertilisers, pesticides and herbicides, get the biggest slice of the subsidy pie.
• Agrichemical manufacturers. Sales would be lower if small family farms prevailed, since they use fewer chemicals.
• Intensive chicken, beef and pork producers. The growth of the cheap meat industry is linked to the growth of the fast-food industry which depends on subsidised animal feed. Without it meat would cost generally more and hamburgers would cost a lot more than 99 pence.

Subsidies v Aid
After military aid, most aid to developing countries is agricultural. Much of it is aimed at increasing – yes, increasing – their reliance on hybrid seeds, agrichemicals and labour-saving

machinery. Recently it has been targeted at supporting the export of biotechnology products. All of these have long-term effects on yields, soil fertility and the rural economy.

The repayment of Third World debt results in a net transfer of resources from struggling South to prosperous North. In 1998 Third World Countries put about $114.6 billion into the private and public coffers of the North. The 41 poorest countries paid $1.7 billion more than they received in aid. Since 1981, the South has transferred to the North $3.7 trillion, and yet today more that $200 billion is still owed. Many countries have to borrow even more in order to repay interest and debt. Governments in the South have had to sacrifice their internal economies, abandon health, education, employment, popular housing, land demarcation for indigenous peoples, agrarian reform and environmental protection in order to keep up payments. Natural resources have been squandered in the attempt to keep up interest payments. Most of the burden of repayment falls on agriculture, an agriculture struggling to survive already against the pressure of prices depressed by US (and other) subsidies.

So you think that your hamburger is cheap

Given the chance, farmers could compete internationally. Third World farmers as well as US and EU family farmers would benefit economically. Disease, overpopulation and poverty would be alleviated by increased domestic and foreign income. The annual income benefit for the developing world could be as much as $1.75 trillion if food prices found their natural unsubsidised level.

Subsidised burgers and chicken nuggets come at an awful cost.

State of the World 2002
Earthscan Worldwatch Institute
ISBN 1 85383 878 0

The Digestive System

chewing it over

The food we eat contains protein, carbohydrate, fats, vitamins and minerals. It also contains other elements that nourish us in ways that are, as yet, not completely understood. If different people eat the same foods some will gain the nutrients they need, other will experience nutrient deficiencies. Why?

We need to look at the 'soil food web'. A plant sends its roots into the soil in search of nutrients as food. In healthy soil there are some 500 known organisms and it is these that provide the nutrients. Plants produce 'exudates', which include sugars that nourish and regulate the balance of life around its root system – while attracting micro-organisms. Other microorganisms are food for other life forms whose excrement provides plant nutrients. A complex symbiosis

exists. It's a plant's 'mycorrhizae', or 'fungus-roots' that ensure this close mutually beneficial relationship between soil and plant roots. Thin white mycorrhizal fungal filaments extend the 'reach' of the roots and enables them to draw nutrients from the furthest parts of the soil. The use of pesticides, fungicides or herbicides devastates soil organism populations. So do nitrate fertilisers, but they compensate by providing concentrated, readily available nutrients direct to the roots. This is why a 'chemical' farmer can adopt chemical use overnight but an organic farmer needs a lot of composting to build up a new soil food web.

So what about digestion? The food we eat is converted into what the Chinese politely call 'night soil' – produced while we sleep and our digestive system works away. It is so similar to soil that many parasitic worms can thrive as well in our intestines as in the soil.

Over 500 different organisms – 'intestinal flora' – weighing a total of 6 lbs, have been identified in our digestive system. The human body also has 'roots' that function in the same way as a plant's roots, delivering nutrients from the 'soil' in the intestines to the rest of the body. These are the intestinal 'villi' – root-like protruberances that pack the small intestine.

The villi are protected from direct contact with food by a layer of mucus composed of intestinal flora, *Lactobacillus acidophilus* in particular. If this protective layer is eroded the villi, packed with tiny capillaries, bleed and are unable to absorb the nutrients that the body needs from the liquefied food. It is intestinal bacteria, such as *Acidophilus*, that carry nutrients to the villi and create others such as B vitamins. They also control undesirable bacteria by secreting natural antibiotics. This is the human 'digestive food web' that has evolved to enable us to exist on a wide variety of foods.

However, there are quite a few ways this can go wrong and they echo the way that the soil food web can be upset by nitrate fertilisers, pesticides and fungicides.

Eating sugar and white flour products encourages yeasts to grow and compete with the *acidophilus* bacteria. Yeasts irritate the villi, creating gases and causing bloating and cramping. The villi are exposed to nutrients that have not been filtered by the layer of flora and absorb unwanted substances that the body must excrete, a condition known as 'malabsorption syndrome'. Antibiotic use eradicates large numbers of intestinal flora, in the same way that fungicides eradicate mycorrhizal fungi. Stress can have a physical effect; the intestines twist with 'anxiety' and internal rubbing removes patches of flora. Other flora-harming substances include alcohol, chlorine in drinking water, cigarettes and preservatives. Milk can cause harm, particularly in lactose-intolerant people.

Maintaining a healthy digestive food web means introducing the same conditions that composting provides to create a healthy soil food web: plenty of organic matter (by consuming leaves and wholegrains), inoculation with the 'right' bacteria (by eating yoghurt, sauerkraut or sourdough bread), careful chewing to ensure small particle sizes, avoidance of substances that harm the desirable bacteria that make up the intestinal flora.

It is extraordinary that, with all our scientific knowledge of nutrition and the human body, we should – millions of us – allow ourselves to be persuaded to eat so badly.

 "As above, so below." Eating organically requires the same understanding and harnessing of natural processes that farming organically requires. Success comes from achieving a healthy bacterial community and in preventing the 'dysbiosis', or system, failure that leads to disease.

Probiotics: Nature's Internal Healers
Natasha Trenev
Avery Publishing Group 1998
ISBN 0 895 29847 3

Obesity

dieting can make you fat

*"I have more flesh than another man, and
therefore more frailty."*
Falstaff, Henry IV: Part One, Shakespeare

If school children were injected with a disease that crippled them, shortened their lifespans and increased their dependency on health services there would be outrage. Yet we watch, helpless, as a combination of heavily advertised junk food and inactivity achieves a similar result through obesity – a condition that is rarely curable.

Children's TV programmes are the main promoters of foods such as sugary breakfast cereals, confectionery, soft drinks and fast food. It is left to 'pester power' to do the rest. If obesity doesn't strike in childhood, modern lifestyles make it a risk at all stages of life. Eating too many calories is half the problem; not burning them off is the other half. Watching television, using cars, living in suburbs that make walking or cycling impractical all combine to reduce calorie usage. So, food is not the only culprit, but it is a major factor.

America claims world leadership in obesity. Fat is epidemic, with an estimated 61 per cent of Americans overweight, of whom 27 per cent are obese. The problem is even more pronounced among the poor, especially Afro-Americans.

Obesity is responsible for 325,000 American deaths annually, more than motor vehicles, illegal drugs, alcohol and firearms combined. Overweight people are more likely than others to die from heart disease, stroke, kidney failure, gallstones, arthritis, pregnancy complications, and depression. It is set to overtake smoking in the US as the leading cause of death and it kills eight times more than die of AIDS.

Beyond the human costs, the financial costs of obesity are staggering: some $117 billion annually in healthcare and lost wages in the US. The 'five-a-day' campaign to encourage Americans to eat more fruit and vegetables spends $2 million a year in promotion. McDonald's spend more than $1 billion and Coca Cola spend $800 million on advertising. Exactly how much encouragement do we need to become obese?

The lawyers who successfully sued 'Big Tobacco' are now suing the fast food and snack industries – known collectively as 'Big Fat'. These companies, the lawyers say, use manipulative strategies to market unhealthy products that, eaten regularly, can lead to disease and death. Concerned nutritionists have called for a 'fat tax' on such food.

So what about dieting? Slimming is rarely successful, even in the short term. If you reduce food intake the rate at which your metabolism burns calories slows down – a natural survival mechanism inherited from our ancestors, whose food supply was uncertain. When you start eating normally again, calories are burned off more slowly and weight accumulates. This is 'yo-yo dieting' and it can lead to net weight gain. Regular exercise helps reduce weight, but obesity makes exertion difficult. Choosing the right foods can help: foods that are high in complex carbohydrates (starch) and fibre help to create the feeling of fullness that stops you overeating and so reduces your calorie intake.

What about non-nutritive, artificial foods that replace sugar and fat? Users of the sweetener, Aspartame, often complain that using it in place of sugar overrides that sense of 'fullness', tempting those who eat 'diet' foods actually to eat more. Similar negative effects can be found with artificial fats, such as 'Olestra'. These have been cleverly developed to escape digestion but the side effect of 'anal leakage' means they are not a success with consumers.

Body Mass Index – BMI

How to calculate:

Body weight in Kgs ÷ height in metres squared = BMI

Over 25 BMI = Overweight

Over 30 BMI = Obese

Example:

Body weight 80 Kgs ÷ height (1.8m) in metres squared 3.24 = 24.69 BMI. Not quite overweight.

Very Fast Food

and the very slow people it creates

"Those who do not have enough time for good health will not have good health enough for time."

Paul Bragg

Americans are getting fat. On any day, one in every four Americans visits a fast food restaurant. The growth of the market for fast food is spectacular – in the US it has gone from $6 billion in 1970 to $110 billion in 2000, nearly 20 times growth. Having saturated the market in the US and Europe, McDonald's is opening branches in China. They now have 28,700 outlets in 120 countries. The startling figures don't just relate to beef, though; consumption of 'french fries' has increased from 4 pounds to 30 pounds per person per year, all cooked in beef tallow or hydrogenated fat (see chapter 40). The soft drinks that are packaged in the 'meal deals' of fast food outlets ensure that a good dose of sugar is consumed with every burger and fries.

Obesity rates have, inevitably, rocketed in line with fast food production. The $320 billion cost of obesity to society is twice the income of the fast food industry. Fast food isn't the only cause of obesity, but the high levels of fat and sugar in a fast food meal are many times greater than those found in home-cooked food or in conventional restaurant food. Levels of dietary fibre and vegetables are much lower. The combination undermines all the health advice of government and nutritional bodies.

Some nutritionists call for a tax on fast food to reduce consumption and also to help pay for the cost of the obesity and illness that fast food generates. Yet Government policy operates in the opposite direction. Their main effect is to keep the price of animal feed, sugar and fats such as rapeseed and soya oil unnaturally cheap. These are the key ingredients of fast food. Take away the subsidies and a burger, cola and fries meal priced at $2.49 would cost $7.50. Cattle feed costs in the US are lower today than they were in 1933, during severe economic depression. Low feed costs, the use of hormones and antibiotics as growth promoters, 'market deficiency' payments, cheap immigrant labour, intensive rearing conditions and special tax breaks all work to keep the cost of a fast food meal extremely low and yet very profitable. No similar basket of payments exists for producers of vegetables or other nutritionally desirable foods. If a fast food meal was priced at its true cost and penalised for its health costs to society then we would see a very different picture. Meanwhile, the industry is praised as an example of popular capitalism while being heavily dependent on state support.

The shiny presentation of fast food restaurants belies another problem: the unsanitary conditions on intensive factory farms that has led to a flurry of foodborne diseases such as E.coli, salmonella and campylobacter. Food poisoning cases in the UK have risen from fewer than 19,000 in 1989 to more than 100,000 in 1999. E.coli has long been a problem, caused by the faecal contamination of beef in the slaughterhouse. Symptoms of contamination are stomach cramps and diarrhoea. However, in 1983 a new, highly toxic form of the bacteria emerged, E.coli O157:H7. Its symptoms include death (200 per year in the US) and kidney failure (see chapter 'Deadly Diseases'). The emergence of this new, deadly form of E.coli coincides with the introduction of intensive feedlot rearing of beef, dependent on continuous feeding of antibiotics.

In Britain the feeding of animal remains to livestock was banned in 1996 as a result of the BSE epidemic among cattle and the risk that it was linked to variant Creutzfeld Jacobs Disease (CJD) among humans. In the US the feeding of sheep, cow, dog and cat remains to cattle was banned in 1997. Yet there are no prohibitions on feeding dead chickens, pigs or horses, or even cattle blood. Cattle remains may be fed to chickens. Chicken manure may be fed to cattle. With practices like these, the spread of disease is inevitable and high-speed slaughterhouse practices, where 'gut table' spillages are commonplace, only increase the risk of contamination further.

The situation is now so dire that we are seeing lawsuits organised by the lawyers who successfully sued tobacco companies. The legal principle, that a manufacturer has a duty to warn consumers of the dangers of their product, has been established. Where will it end and to what extent will government intervene to control this run-away industry?

One of the largest beneficiaries of US government subsidies is Archer Daniels Midland (ADM), a leading processor of animal products and supplier of ingredients to the fast-food industry. In a secretly recorded conversation the president of the company commented, at a price-fixing meeting with Japanese executives: "Our competitors are our friends, our customers are our enemies".

The vice-chairman of ADM was sent to prison in 1999 for price-fixing on lysine (a chicken feed additive made from subsidised corn). This was after they had been fined heavily for fixing prices on corn syrup, an essential sweetener in the US. It is, of course, subsidised, as is the corn from which it is made.

In the UK an estimated 5.5 million people a year are affected by food poisoning. Of those 71% believed their food-borne illness was caused as a result of eating in a restaurant, cafe or fast food outlet.

More than 1 billion adults worldwide are affected by obesity with approximately 500,000 people in the US and Western Europe dying from obesity-related diseases each year.

Fast Food Nation
Eric Schlosser
Allen Lane 2001
ISBN 0 713 99602 1

Intensive Agriculture

how intense can you get?

One hundred thousand years ago the Earth lived on its natural wealth: rich soils produced food for plants that fed animals that fed predators. The hunting to extinction of large mammals was the first step towards the loss of the Earth's resources. Domestication of grazing animals and the use of fire led to the destruction of forests and creation of pasture. Agriculture followed, giving rise to the growth of civilisations, beginning in Sumer in the Tigris-Euphrates river system. Sumer's richly productive irrigated land, however, eventually became saline and eroded. Over a span of 2,500 years the world's first culture rose, flourished, then disappeared from history. In our own time, the last 50 years in the US has seen 55 million acres lost to salination. The 'heartland' states, where intensified industrial agriculture dominates, are losing 5–10 tonnes of topsoil per acre each year.

Such an outcome is brought on by the 'cascade effect' of agricultural deterioration; all of which starts with nitrates, the key chemical fertiliser.

In the cascade effect:
- nitrates wipe out nitrogen-fixing bacteria in soil and encourage bacteria that break down organic matter and humus

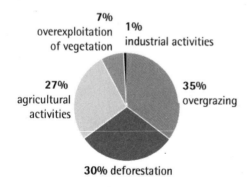

7% overexploitation of vegetation

1% industrial activities

27% agricultural activities

35% overgrazing

30% deforestation

Causes of soil erosion

- loss of humus leads to reduced water retention, meaning more irrigation is needed
- without humus, nutrients are washed away and life in the soil declines, the soil turns acid and more organic matter is destroyed
- the soil no longer holds together, salts build up and erosion increases and quickens at up to 17 times the rate at which it is formed.
- the depleted soils require ever larger inputs of chemicals to produce decreasing levels of yields
- more fertiliser encourages more weed growth, requiring increased herbicide applications
- fertiliser encourages fast but weak and sappy growth, making plants vulnerable to insect and fungal attack. Insecticides and fungicides are needed to save the crop
- insecticides indiscriminately wipe out most insects, pests and pollinators, reducing biodiversity both above and below ground.
- herbicides wash into the water supply, giving rise to increased cancer rates and hormonal changes in wildlife and humans that lead to birth defects, gender imbalance and developmental problems
- plant and animal species become extinct
- nitrous oxide, a greenhouse gas, is generated

from fertilised fields while nitrous acid contributes to acid rain
- the reduced water retention in soil leads to rapid runoff and flooding after heavy rains.

None of the costs of these side effects of industrial agriculture are charged back to the perpetrators.

Intensified animal production – factory farming – has brought its own problems: widespread diseases that have developed new levels of virulence and antibiotic resistance and skyrocketing rates of food poisoning. Foodborne illness in the US, according to the Center for Disease Control, now kills 9,000 people a year. UK reported cases of food poisoning rose 500 per cent between 1988 and 1998. Animal husbandry, the relationship between the producer and the domestic food animal, has been replaced by levels of animal suffering without historical precedent.

Alongside all this, subsidies to 'efficient' modern intensive agriculture have never been higher in Europe or the US. The real cost to the taxpayer of subsidies and cleaning up the mess intensive agriculture causes is estimated to be equal to 40 per cent on the average family's food bill, or about £30 per week.

Pesticide usage creates alarming figures. In 1990, the WHO estimated that there were 3 million acute pesticide poisonings in the developing world, of which 220,000 were fatal. Revised figures indicate 25 million poisoning cases. In the US 20,000 farmworkers suffer acute pesticide poisoning every year. **Pesticides and herbicides 'bioaccumulate', moving up the food chain, often ending up in mothers' milk.**

The destruction of habitat by monoculture reduces environmental niches. Extinction is the result, perhaps even of species that have not yet been discovered. Communities themselves suffer extinction in the face of intensification. Rural population declines, communities and the businesses that serve them collapse.

But that's what we have to do to feed ourselves, say many experts. The world, to them, is not too high a price to pay for human survival.

An agricultural monocultural system that can't make money without subsidies, washes away the land, undermines biodiversity and is dependent on fossil fuels for its machinery and chemicals is unsustainable... and inefficient. **The sole justification of agricultural intensification has been based on falsified costings.**

Small farms produce more food per hectare or acre than large farms; they just do it with more people and lower chemical inputs. A large monoculture farm may produce more corn per acre, but this crude measure doesn't take into account the livestock on a small farm that provide food and manure, bees that pollinate and provide honey, and the fewer chemicals used. Many small farms 'intercrop', planting a secondary crop between the rows of a main crop, operating with a flexibility not available to monoculture. The 1992 US Agricultural census described the 'Inverse Farm Size-Productivity Relationship' and showed that farms under 27 acres were ten times more productive in cash output per acre than farms larger than 6,000 acres. Even the World Bank now supports smaller-scale farming and encourages land reform to place small farmers on inefficient large landholdings. True 'intensification' of agriculture is when a farmer is in intimate contact with the land, the wildlife and the environment and maximises only output sustainably.

So why is corporate industrialised farming so powerful?

- someone else pays the true cost of environmental damage, loss of biodiversity and harm to human health
- a greater proportion of subsidies goes to the largest farms
- many big farms belong to multinationals which can operate at a loss because their real profit comes from trading and processing the farm produce. They also receive tax breaks that smaller farmers do not
- government policy makers are the natural allies of the large oil, chemical, pharmaceutical and agricultural equipment lobbyists. So are 'industrial' farmers.

Consumers and taxpayers pay the price for lower quality food and a deteriorating environment. If the true cost of food were transparent, if polluters had to pay for the harm they caused and if soil was seen as an asset that had to be preserved for future generations, then industrial agriculture would end.

Fatal Harvest: The Tragedy of Industrial Agriculture
Andrew Kimbrell (Ed)
Island Press 2002
ISBN 1 55963 941 5

Deadly Diseases

the bomb ticks on

In Victorian Britain the discovery of pathogenic bacteria led to the creation of London's sewer system. Removing people from contact with their own excrement was the most effective way to reduce levels of diseases such as typhoid and cholera. The world agreed and sewerage systems around the globe were modelled on London's example.

However, in modern agriculture exposing animals to the excrement of their fellows is commonplace. The crowded conditions of cattle lead to the contamination of beef and milk with E.Coli O157:H7. Feeding poultry manure to cattle for extra protein leads to the development of salmonella. In the US the amounts of manure from farm animals is 10 times that produced by the human population and bypasses the usual sanitation system, making it the single largest cause of river pollution. After hamburgers, waterborne contamination is the next largest cause of E. Coli infection.

Chicken in cages stacked on wire mesh floors drop excrement onto their neighbours below. 'People want cheap chicken,' argue the producers. In Sweden the government announced that if salmonella was found on chicken farms the entire flock would be slaughtered. So, chicken farmers cleaned up and salmonella was eliminated. The extra cost of running a clean system is estimated at $8 million per year. The saving to the health system is $28 million. Most salmonella cases in Sweden now occur with returning tourists who picked up the infection abroad. Swedish chicken sells at a premium in other Nordic countries.

In England in late 1988, Junior Health Minister Edwina Currie remarked that "most of the egg production in this country" was contaminated with salmonella, and urged us to cook eggs thoroughly. Egg sales fell and she was sacked. Two months later, a confidential government

report was leaked. It stated that up to two million infections a year result from the eating of eggs and chickens in the UK. Between one third and two thirds of all chickens were infected.

A BMA report stated that the number of cases of food poisoning was at its highest ever in 1997. "The only safe approach for the food industry and general public is to treat all raw meat as infected," the BMA report urged. One million people were estimated to be infected by salmonella or E. Coli 0157 bacteria; 200 people died. Reported cases in 1998 exceeded 100,000, up from 20,000 in 1988. The Food Standards Agency in 2001 set an aim to reduce cases of food poisoning by 20 per cent by 2005 – back to 1990s levels; hardly progress. The responsibility for hygiene remains, oddly, the consumer's rather than the producer's.

However, antibiotics have made it possible to keep sick animals alive in these grim conditions, allowing pathogens to develop resistance. These mutations have brought suffering and death to consumers around the world.

In June 2001 ConAgra, one of the world's largest agribusiness corporations, recalled 19 million pounds (76 million hamburgers) of E.coli-contaminated beef that was produced on intensive feed lots and slaughtered in their highly mechanised slaughterhouses. The Denver Post commented: "If 19 million pounds of meat distributed to half of this country had been contaminated with a deadly strain of E. coli bacteria by terrorists, we'd go nuts. But when it's done by a Fortune 100 corporation, we continue to buy it and feed it to our kids".

There are 61 deaths and 73,000 cases of E. coli 0157:H7 poisoning in the U.S. every year. In Britain, where fewer than 60 people have died of the human variant of mad cow disease in the past decade, the entire beef industry was nearly closed down.

"It's time for the Congress to take a good, hard look at food safety policies," said Wenonah Hauter, director of Public Citizen's Critical Mass Energy and Environment Program. "The ConAgra recall is not an aberration. It is another example of a food safety system that is teetering on the brink of collapse."

The Swedes have shown that faecal contamination and the spread of disease are not inevitable in meat production. Better hygiene led to the elimination of typhoid and cholera in Victorian Britain. By not applying the same understanding to our food production we have simply replaced water-borne faecal diseases with new food-borne faecal diseases. The principle of prevention as applied to human sewage has not been applied to meat production and consumers pay the price in disease, disability and death.

The FAO has stated that cattle fed on pasture have 1/100th the level of E.coli 0157:H7 as cattle fed on concentrated food such as corn, soy and ground up animal products. Organic cattle feed on pasture and hay. Organic chickens are not stacked up and exposed to faecal contamination.

It Was Probably Something You Ate: A Practical Guide to Avoiding and Surviving Foodborne Illness
Nicols Fox
Penguin 1999
ISBN 0 140 27799 4

The (Not-so?) Green Revolution

when 'green' isn't good

Norman Borlaug, the 'Father of the Green Revolution', which was brought to the developing world back in the 1970s, has called for a 'Second Green Revolution'. But do we need another one? What was the first and how successful was it?

Back in the 60s, amidst dire warnings of global famines, Borlaug developed his 'miracle wheat' that was set to change grain yields in some of the world's most vulnerable countries.

The Green Revolution depended on short-stalk wheat and rice. Grain crops naturally grow on stalks that are several feet high, supported by strong root structures. The high plant shades out competition from weeds and also provides straw for animal bedding, thatching and other uses. New hybrid varieties developed had very short stalks and limited root networks, thus allowing the plant to concentrate its energy on seed production. As long as plenty of chemical weedkillers and fertilisers were applied bigger crops could be harvested. Mechanisation also helped to increase yields.

This new crop came to India and, indeed, where food shortages had once been forecast, yields of cereal grains went up and India began to export wheat. But the news had a sting in its tail. Between 1970 and 1990 (the two decades of major Green Revolution advances) the number of hungry people in the world actually went up from 536 million to 597 million. The mere existence of food has never been a guarantee that everyone eats. If it were then there would be no hunger in the United States or India, both food exporting-countries. Poverty is the main cause of hunger; loss of land to grow food on is the other.

Back in India, the practicalities of the Green Revolution were hard for smaller farmers. They couldn't afford the new seeds and chemicals so were forced off their land while larger farmers prospered. Chemicals replaced labour; small farmers and farm labourers joined the ranks of the unemployed and hungry. The fertility and humus content of the soil fell. This decline in fertility meant farmers in India had to use more and more fertiliser each year just to maintain the same yields. Profit margins were squeezed as higher yields brought falling prices against a background of higher fertiliser cost.

As the fertility and mineral content of the soil have fallen, so have the levels of iron, zinc and Vitamin A in the food produced. Anaemia and other deficiency diseases abound. These losses counteract any gains in carbohydrate availability. Consumption of fruits, vegetables and legumes has also fallen. In Bangladesh before the Green Revolution, there were over 100 types of green plants that flourished alongside rice in the paddies providing dietary betacarotenes, iron and folic acid. The use of herbicides has killed these plants. Rice production increased, but extra blindness, anaemia and birth defects resulted from the loss of these supplementary foods. **There are six million children who die each year of malnutrition. India and Bangladesh share a high proportion of that figure.**

Was the Green Revolution worth it? In 1993 a study of farms in South India found that the productivity and profitability of 'ecological farms' was equal to that of chemical-intensive farms who followed the Green Revolution. Profits, however, were shared among a larger number of people in 'ecological farms'. Soil erosion and depletion of fertility were all higher on the intensive farms.

The Green Revolution has gone flat. Norman Borlaug hopes that a 'Second Green Revolution' will be based on genetic engineering – that modified crops will one day deliver higher yields with lower fertiliser and pesticide inputs. Engineering crops to grow in saline soil is part of

this dream. His call is enthusiastically supported by chemical companies such as Monsanto, Novartis, and Dupont, as well as the World Bank and other international agencies. Hunger and starvation can only be beaten with the tools of biotechnology, they claim. So far all progress has been theoretical with the word 'might' used alongside all the anticipated miracles of genetic engineering since the 1980s. For the 5,000 children a day who die of malnutrition in India that is small comfort.

- The regions of Andhra Pradesh and Punjab, India's two leading agricultural regions, suffer high rates of agricultural suicide as farmers struggle to meet crippling interest rates on grain and chemical purchases.

- Irrigated and chemically fertilised land suffers salination and has to be taken out of production. Six per cent of India's agricultural land is now useless and the rate of loss is increasing. That loss is not caused by 'ecological' farming.

- A farmer using pesticides and fertilisers uses 12 calories of energy from fossil fuels to produce one calorie of food energy. A subsistence farmer with a hoe uses one calorie of energy to produce 20 calories of food. A sustainable 'revolution' lies somewhere between these extremes of high and low-tech farming.

Agri-Culture
Jules Pretty
Earthscan 2002
ISBN 1 85383 925 6

Food Miles and the Food Chain

going far?

In the 19th century, when oranges were only available for a few months of the year, wealthy country-house owners built large greenhouses, or orangeries, to extend the season for these luxury goods. Now, thanks to cheap fuel, yesterday's luxuries are today's 'commodities' and oranges and orange juice are available all the year round. But have we gone too far?

Fossil fuels are the foundation of our modern food supply. Cheap oil is an essential ingredient in the manufacture of chemical fertilisers, pesticides and as fuel for agricultural machinery. Once food has left the farm, high levels of fuel are used to transport it long distances before it reaches the consumer. This system is, oddly, promoted as 'efficient'; and it assumes that fossil fuel supplies are infinite and that oil prices will remain stable. The true cost of transporting food over great distances, however, is not that low, particularly if we consider the massive future costs of global warming, caused by CO_2 emissions and oil shortages.

Transport by road and by air uses up lots of fuel – the 'cheapness' of which is artificial. Roads are built by governments using taxpayers' money and then provided 'free' for transport use. Aviation fuel is untaxed, giving air freight a strong competitive advantage. An airline pays 18p per litre for fuel, while a road-transport company must pay 80p. Air freight burns 50 litres of fuel to carry the amount of food for which a ship would burn one litre, or road transport six litres. Without such 'subsidised' road and air transport, a very different pattern of food growing and distribution would emerge.

"UK imports of food and animal feed currently use 1.6 billion litres of fuel and produce 4.1 million tonnes of carbon dioxide emissions. More than one third of all truck traffic on Britain's roads is carrying food. By the time it reaches the supermarkets and shops food production and distribution has produced eight tonnes of carbon dioxide emissions per household. This amount is matched by the eight tonnes of CO_2 emissions of the average household from their house and family car.

(Note that the 2001 foot and mouth disease epidemic in Britain showed that the spread of the disease was assisted by the transport of live animals around the country and that imports of meat from abroad may have been the source of infection.)

So what's the solution?

The WTO opposes any 'restraint' on free global trade. Any tariff barriers against imported food would be struck down as unfair and anti-competitive. But there are other ways to reduce food miles.

There is already a growing trend towards localised food systems with farmers' markets, box schemes and community-supported agriculture. Leading supermarkets in Britain announced in July

2002 their commitment to sourcing more food locally and, in the case of Sainsbury's, to phasing out all imported beef and milk by 2005. The more customers appreciate the benefits of fresh, locally produced food, the more food miles are saved. Seasonal foods are also better appreciated now. Anyone who has tasted fresh homegrown asparagus knows that no price discount can make the imported alternative taste better. The term 'imported' could finally be losing its cachet.

Environmental taxes on aviation fuel and petrol would help tip the balance in favour of local and regional produce. Unfortunately, any taxes that threaten the public's love affair with air travel and the motor car will be politically fraught. It's a conundrum: we care about our environment yet don't want to abandon our pleasures. Subsidising local production and setting targets for increasing domestic production would, perhaps, prove less politically sensitive.

In the 1970s UK fruit producers were subsidised to grub out apple trees. Half of Britain's apple orchards disappeared. Imports from Chile, South Africa, the USA, New Zealand and Europe, often coated in preservative fungicides such as Captan or diphenylamine, filled the gap. The consequent loss to the British rural economy hinged on a few pence per pound saving on cheaper imports. In 2002 local fruit production begun making a (Government-subsidised) comeback. Consumer taste has moved on from the days when Golden Delicious was the popular ideal.

You might as well eat oil

The Food Miles Report: the dangers of long-distance food transport
Angela Paxton
SAFE Alliance 1994
ISBN 1 899 77905 1

Supermarkets

taking control

The self-service store is a recent addition to our high streets, made possible through the advances in food processing and packaging of the 1950s. No longer tied to the bacon slicer and the cheese wire, grocers concentrated on stocking the shelves and taking the money. Just one problem: Retail Price Maintenance (RPM). Prices were legally fixed so that Heinz could, for example, print the price of 11d on a tin of beans and insist on it. It was Tesco Stores, under the leadership of 'Stack it high, sell it cheap' founder Jack Cohen, who challenged the law in 1964 by selling foods at lower prices. An embarrassed Government found it difficult to intervene to keep the cost of food high and RPM was abandoned. The new 'supermarkets' were free to negotiate lower prices from suppliers and so shift the balance of power from the producer to the retailer. The consumer – the retailer's primary route to profit – liked it. The pressure on suppliers for cheapness led to corner-cutting, particularly in meat production, where what the buyer didn't see they didn't know – until salmonella, E.coli and BSE appeared and the true cost of bargain prices was highlighted.

By the 1970s just five supermarkets controlled more than half the total food sales in Britain. **It was said that 15 men decided what the other 55 million people in Britain ate.** It wasn't quite that simple – but those 15 men did have immense power and dictated what appeared on the shelves: the brand leader, the number 2 and the supermarket own-label version. Any brand that didn't make the grade either disappeared or reinvented itself as a 'delicatessen' brand to carve out a niche in specialist food shops. Small independent grocers went out of business in droves. As supermarkets expanded to provide hardware, clothing, housewares, chemist products, newspapers and magazines their impact affected retailers in all sectors. The out-of-town superstores changed petrol retailing took off as fickle motorists travelled further to stock up on food and fuel at the same location. The desire for year-round availability led to rising food imports, which often replaced domestic production, with costs to the domestic economy as well as increased fossil fuel usage.

The supermarkets' influence is also a psychological one. Walk in and the first thing you see is fresh produce. This sets the consumer's impression of the whole store. After fruit and veg the other perishable foods that shoppers regularly buy are bread and milk. These are usually found at the opposite end of the store, requiring shoppers to cross the entire store. 'Impulse purchases' are encouraged by placing selected items at the end of aisles. Deep price discounts on 'Known Value Items' (KVI) such as milk, sliced bread and baked beans cash in on research showing that consumers only know what the few most popular food items actually cost. By making sure these always look cheap, supermarkets create the overall impression of low prices without giving too much away.

Organic and high quality food

By the late 1990s supermarkets had developed 'loyalty cards' which provided details on consumer preferences. One of the first discoveries was that consumers who bought just one organic item were likely to spend twice as much as other shoppers per store visit. These are the consumers that supermarkets want – those who are concerned with quality rather than price. No sooner had they identified these customers, than the supermarkets noticed they were visiting the stores less often. Organic 'box schemes' – giving customers a weekly home delivery of seasonal vegetables – were blamed. In response, in June of 1998, Waitrose relaunched its organic offering, with 300 different organic lines. Sainsbury's followed in July and Tesco weighed in a few months later. The leading stores of Southeast England were taking organic food seriously and demand surged, by as much as 35 per cent growth per annum, to the delight of organic farmers and processors. By 2002 both Waitrose and Sainsbury's could claim 2,000 organic lines, moving these items onto the mainstream shelves to compete with the 'big boys'. Some natural food stores benefited from increased awareness of organics., but the village shop and other small independent retailers couldn't compete and many disappeared, weakening the fabric of rural communities. **The knock-on effect in the community of a new supermarket opening is a net loss of 260 jobs.**

Supermarkets quickly woke up to the new trend for valuing high-quality food above cheapness. With the food scares of BSE, salmonella, E.Coli, listeria and Foot and Mouth there is a continuing flight to quality and the supermarkets are leading the charge, eager to escape the trap of ever-reducing prices and profit margins. Their latest challenge, as demanded by customers, is to increase the amount of locally produced foods. Sainsbury's have assigned employees to develop regional sourcing. After eliminating diversity in the 1960s, supermarkets now actively develop local and regional producers, many of them organic, in an attempt to keep up with evolving tastes.

The balance of power has shifted: no longer do 15 male supermarket buyers decide what we eat. Every purchase at the till is a vote recorded for a particular product, and if supermarkets ignore their customers they will shop elsewhere. The big supermarkets still have a long way to go to prove their commitment to local and organic produce. At the moment 70 per cent of total UK organic supermarket supplies are imported, offering little benefit to the UK-supplier. But they are making progress (see chart below). Let us hope they also learn to support suppliers rather than squeeze them, and that small-scale producers will be able to flourish.

Supermarket	% Organic imports	Notes
Waitrose	15%	Aims to source 100% from UK when in season
M&S	40%	Imports in some areas as low as 3% (diary)
Sainsbury	60%	Target to reduce imports to 45% by 2004
Co-op	66%	-
Safeway	75%	All standard organic potatoes now from UK
Tesco	80%	-

(Sustain July 2002)

Since the 1960s the proportion of income spent on food has dropped from 25% to 10%, while real incomes have gone up. All the data suggests that supermarkets must provide the customer with organic, high-quality, locally sourced food if they are to regain a larger share of people's spending.

Tastes Familiar

fooling your taste buds

We all learnt in school that there are four tastes: sweet, salty, sour and bitter. There's another taste, however, that is the favourite of food technologists and mass caterers. It's called '*umami*' and translates as 'meaty' or 'savoury' and is conveyed by several naturally occurring substances, including glutamate – an amino acid present in protein-rich foods.

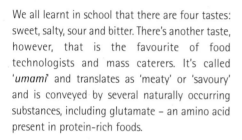

Umami was always a part of Japanese cuisine, with '*dashi kombu*' or seaweed broth, used as the base for miso soup, noodle broth and other staples. In Europe *umami* is tasted in chicken stock, beef extract and aged cheeses such as Cheddar. Sun-ripened tomatoes, mushrooms, baby peas or freshly picked sweet corn all have small quantities of glutamic acid that turns into more complex, but less flavoursome, proteins as the vegetable ripens. That's why we pick them young, while the flavour is at its peak – a signal that nutritious proteins are present.

Back in the 1920s Japanese scientist Kikunae Ikeda studied kombu seaweed and isolated the glutamic acid molecule that was the essence of umami flavour. He developed a cheap way to get glutamic acid crystallising it and manufacturing its salt, monosodium glutamate (MSG) and then founded the Ajinomoto Corporation, the world's leading manufacturer of artificial flavourings and sweeteners. Vast quantities of MSG are now made using acid hydrolysis. A protein source, (usually defatted soybean meal), is boiled in hydrochloric acid. The acid breaks down the proteins, some of which form glutamic acid.

MSG use spread worldwide. From being an unacknowledged element in people's diet, MSG attained unprecedented levels of consumption. No research into MSG's safety was done before adding it to the food supply – people didn't bother with such things back then.

But by the 1970s the 'Chinese Restaurant Syndrome' had emerged – numbness, palpitations, headaches and abdominal pains after eating large quantities of MSG. People with allergies or asthma were found to react adversely to small quantities of MSG because glutamic acid also acts as a neurotransmitter in the brain. In babies, as well as unborn babies, glutamic acid passes the brain blood barrier, causing damage to the brain and nervous system. It is now banned in baby foods. It could also pass the barrier in people with hypertension, low blood sugar, diabetes, Alzheimer's, infections and strokes.

The FDA estimates that 2% of the US population is MSG reactive; others put sensitivity to MSG as high as 15–20% – that's about 50,000,000 people; Dr. George Schwartz, author of *In Bad Taste: The MSG Symptom Complex*, believes the numbers are much higher, perhaps 40–50%.

Even a healthy person, having consumed three grammes of MSG on an empty stomach, could develop MSG-related symptoms. A serving of a typical meal with food containing glutamate has only half a gramme of MSG, so a healthy person would have to eat six servings before feeling effects. Some snack foods, however, such as dry-roasted nuts, flavoured potato crisps and extruded puffed snacks, have much higher levels of MSG. So in one quick snack the high doses of MSG trigger a rapid increase in blood glutamate levels and adverse affects are likely to be experienced more quickly and intensely.

If MSG were invented today it would probably not gain approval for use in food. It is, however, now universal. The MSG industry has set up the Glutamate Association to fund research into defending the safety of their product at a time when negative opinion threatens to lead to it being banned, or, at least, to being clearly labelled on food products and restaurant menus.

Instead MSG is hidden under many names: 'Hydrolysed vegetable protein', 'plant protein extract', 'natural flavouring', 'seasoning', 'spices', or 'vegetable bouillon'. MSG can also be an ingredient of an ingredient and so avoid listing.

Good food tastes good without the need for chemical aids. The use of MSG in its various guises has enabled processors and producers to create cheap, flavourless food and cover up its deficiencies with MSG and artificial flavourings. Worse, because of the palate's instinctive attraction to glutamic acid, the use of MSG seduces our tastes away from wholesome food to less natural alternatives.

In the late 60s some Chinese restaurants would put a pot of MSG on tables for diners to sprinkle on their food.

Organic food regulations prohibit the use of MSG, hydrolysed protein or any ingredient which contains MSG.

In Bad Taste: The MSG Symptom Complex
George R. Schwartz
Health Press (NM) 1999
ISBN: 0-929173-30-9

Excitotoxins: The Taste That Kills
Russell L. Blaylock, M.D.
Health Press (NM), 1994
ISBN 0-929173-25-2

The ASA Story

banning truth about healthy eating

What do we really know about the food we eat? The Advertising Standards Authority (ASA) was set up to protect consumers from misleading or factually inaccurate advertising. It is made up of people from the media, the advertising industry and the advertisers themselves and its mission statement is that advertising should be 'legal, decent, honest and truthful'. Adverts making a health claim present a particular challenge and, to avoid controversy, the ASA tends to side with food ads that make no health claims – ie. the least healthy eating options. A few examples will show how advertisers can be muzzled.

Hydrogenated Fat – truth behind the issue

In 1993 Whole Earth Foods launched Superspread™, an alternative to butter and margarine. It was an oil-in-water emulsion rather than a water-in-oil emulsion, similar to mayonnaise, but made with soya instead of eggs and with a buttery flavour. It was launched soon after the publication of Harvard Professor Willett's study (e.g. in *The Lancet*) that verified that hydrogenated fat should not be included in the human food chain because of its high content of unnatural 'trans fats' (See chapter 'Hydrogenation of Fat'). Whole Earth placed an advertisement in *Food Magazine*, a widely respected publication read by nutritionists, dieticians and food technologists in which the case, with detailed evidence, against consuming hydrogenated fats, was set out. BBC2 Food and Drink programme and Channel 4 *Dispatches* both ran programmes about hydrogenated fat and the harm it was doing to the nation's health.

Unilever, the manufacturer of Flora Margarine, has spent millions over the years advertising its own product as 'heart-healthy'. Flora would ensure, it suggested, that hubby survived to see his kids grow up, playing on the housewife's guilt about feeding her man unhealthy food.

Unilever complained to the ASA about the Whole Earth advertisement.

The ASA took action against Whole Earth Foods for 'exploiting consumer fears'. Whole Earth made the point that, if a food was harmful to health, people were bound to be worried. They argued that the ad was factual and based on sound science. The ASA found against Whole Earth, who then appealed. During the appeal period it was noted that Flora's hydrogenated fat content was being reduced. Surely, Whole Earth claimed, this was an admission that its own health warnings must be true. The ASA were unmoved; for them the real offense was that a health issue had been discussed in public. By July of 1993 Flora had reduced the hydrogenated fat in their spread (gradually, so that customers wouldn't notice the change) from 21 per cent to less than one per cent. They then labelled the tubs 'Less than one per cent trans fats' in an appeal to customers conscious of avoiding trans fats. The ASA did nothing.

Organic health claims banned

In 1999 Tesco launched their organic range under the banner of eating a more healthy diet. Geoffrey Hollis, a retired civil servant who headed MAFF's Pesticides Division – responsible for the approval of the pesticides used in British agriculture (quite a few of which have since been banned as carcinogens) complained to the ASA. Tesco, with advice from the Soil Association, set

out the case for proving health claims for organic food: no pesticide residues, higher vitamin and mineral content, no processing treatments, no additives, hormone or antibiotic residues. The ASA ruled against Tesco.

It would appear that the ASA has a policy of inflexibility – if the words 'organic' and 'health' appear in the same advertisement then it is banned. They are proactive against this – they don't wait for complaints. As the organic movement was founded on the belief that health should be its central principle, the ASA policy stops it from communicating its essential message. The food industry spends billions advertising sugar-rich, fatty 'junk' foods, often on children's television where children can barely distinguish the cartoon programme they are watching from advertisements for sugary foods.

A July 2001 report from Sustain, an alliance of campaigners for better food and farming, suggests that up to 99 per cent of adverts for food during children's commercial TV are for products high in fat, sugar or salt.

The ASA was founded to protect consumers from misleading advertising and to protect the advertising industry from Government regulation. In practice ASA policy stops consumers knowing enough to help them make an informed decision on the food – healthy or otherwise – that they choose to eat. The results are apparent.

New guidelines for organic advertisers, produced in July 2001 by the Committee of Advertising Practice (CAP), aim "to create a level playing field for advertisers and help to ensure consumer confidence in this expanding market". One such guideline states: "Advertisers should not claim that organic food is safer or healthier than conventional food unless they have convincing evidence that that is the case. Neither the ASA nor CAP is aware of any such evidence".

The Committee of Advertising Practice
www.cap.org.uk

Sweet Nothings

the truth about sugar

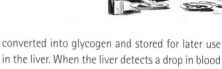

The average American eats 145 pounds of sugar every year – that's about 28 teaspoons per day. At the beginning of the 20th century sugar was still a rare luxury, with average consumption levels at around five pounds per year, less than one teaspoon per day. This spectacular 2,800 per cent rise in sugar consumption is one of the most significant changes in our modern diet.

Sugar from sugar cane is one of our oldest foods, originating in India 5,000 years ago. Before its introduction to the West by Crusaders, honey and fruit were our occasional and seasonal sources of simple sugars such as sucrose, glucose and fructose. It was Christopher Columbus who carried a sugar cane plant to the Caribbean, and slave labour ensured that it remained cheap.

Sugar is sucrose, a combination of one glucose and one fructose molecule. Glucose is the only sugar that our body can use directly. Fructose is converted into glycogen and stored for later use in the liver. When the liver detects a drop in blood sugar level glycogen is converted into glucose.

How is sugar converted to fat?

We should have about 80 calories of glucose (three teaspoons) in our blood and another 300 calories stored as glycogen. We need at least 600 calories a day just to keep going. The backup supply comes from body fat, where a further 100,000 calories are on standby, ready to be converted quickly into glucose. This interchangeability – converting sugars into fats and vice versa – gives us great flexibility and means we can survive on a wide range of foods.

How does sugar make you fat?

When we have a sudden intake of sugar, say a canned soft drink that contains 100 calories or four teaspoons of sugars, two or three teaspoons of glucose go straight into the bloodstream, doubling the blood sugar level. The pancreas releases insulin into the blood to mop up excess sugars, some of which are converted to fats and put into storage. If more sugar is eaten, the fat has little chance to get converted back into sugar and so accumulates. Obesity is a sign that there is more than the 100,000 calories worth of fat that a healthy person needs in reserve.

Insulin Resistance Syndrome and Diabetes

Continued and sudden intakes of sugar lead to frequent insulin releases into the bloodstream. This leads to 'insulin resistance syndrome' where it takes more and more insulin to get the blood sugar level back down to normal. The pancreas continues to produce insulin and too much blood sugar is mopped up, resulting in 'hypoglycemia', or low blood sugar, the symptoms of which are stress, tiredness, anxiety and cravings for sweet foods. The pancreas produces as much insulin as it can, but eventually burns out and stops producing insulin at all. Type II diabetes is the result. When diabetes accompanies high blood pressure and obesity, heart disease usually follows. High sugar consumption, inactivity, stress and smoking all greatly increase the risk of obesity, heart attack and stroke.

And then there's our teeth. Sugar is the main cause of dental decay and gum disease. Toothbrushing can help, as does fluoride, but by far the most effective way to prevent decay is to avoid sugar, or to consume it rarely and only with meals. It has also been shown that cancer cells thrive on glucose. Some therapies work by starving the cancerous cells of sugar.

So, it's the 'surges' in blood glucose level that cause most of the trouble, rather than the sugar itself. Indeed, one of the key functions of blood is to carry sugar, in the form of glucose, around the body. The brain uses more than 300 calories a day, up to half of the glucose in the bloodstream. When the blood sugar level is low, the brain cells, muscles and nerves of the body cannot function correctly and fatigue, irritability, nervousness and faintness result. In extreme forms it exists as bad temper, neurotic behaviour and paranoia.

Sugar displaces more nutritious foods

Sugar satisfies a need for calories but eating more wholesome foods would mean vitamins, minerals, fibre, antioxidants and other micronutrients would also be gained – all of which encourage good health and a strong immune function. Artificial sweeteners such as aspartame, cyclamates and saccharin are equally undesirable (see chapter 'Obesity'). They may replace the calories of sugar, but they can also cause health problems. There is an alternative. The leaves of *Stevia rebaudiana*, a Brazilian plant, produce stevioside, a non-calorific natural sweetener, but lobbying by the manufacturers of other sweeteners has blocked its approval.

Thus, keeping blood sugar levels even is the key to preventing cardiovascular disease, diabetes, obesity, tooth decay and cancer. But sugar is so genuinely addictive that many people struggle with their craving for it.

The safest way to eat sugar is in small quantities with foods that will delay its rapid assimilation and so reduce the extreme swings in blood sugar, energy level and mood: high-fibre foods, for example, such as wholemeal bread, pulses, vegetables and whole cereal products. Apple crumble will have a far milder impact than a glass of apple juice with the same level of sugars.

Without sugar and oxygen, our food and breath, we would die in minutes. Sugar certainly makes many food taste better. But too much of this particular good thing can wreak havoc.

In 1942, when annual production of fizzy soft drinks was about 60 12-ounce servings per person, the American Medical Association's (AMA) Council on Foods and Nutrition stated: "The Council believes it would be in the interest of the public health for all practical means to be taken to limit consumption of sugar in any form in which it fails to be combined with significant proportions of other foods of high nutritive quality."

Today, Americans consume on average ten times the 1942 level of soft drinks and the rest of the world is fast catching up.

The Schwarzbein Principle: The Truth About Weight Loss, Health and Aging
Diana Schwarzbein, Nancy Deville
Health Communications 1999
ISBN 1 558 74680 3

Commodity Markets

reality distorted

The dollar turnover of the largest corporations exceeds that of many of the world's countries. So, a democracy, such as Chile, can be dominated easily by commercial interests. These, inevitably, place the interests of Chile's voters low in their list of priorities.

It is, perhaps, even more alarming that America's largest corporations are far richer and more powerful than US government departments such as the US Department of Agriculture, the Environment Protection Agency and the Food and Drug Administration. With power divided among 50 states, individual Senators and Congressmen, particularly those who chair important committees, can have inordinate power. The voter, even the political party, is often sidelined in this process.

In 1950 25 per cent of US tax income came from corporations. That figure is now 10 per cent.

'Corporate Welfare', giving public money to corporations, was not even discussed in 1950. In 1960, when President Eisenhower handed over power to John Kennedy, he warned against yielding to pressure for wasteful public funding of agriculture and applied research. (In other words, against a system of unsustainable subsidies). He warned that, "In the councils of government, we must guard against the acquisition of unwarranted influence by the military-industrial complex. The potential for the disastrous rise of misplaced power exists and will persist".

What is 'misplaced power?' It is not power that derives from the open market; it has been granted, instead, by government to big business. It excludes smaller companies, which must watch helplessly as their big competitors are helped to become even bigger. The level of consolidation in military and food industries now rivals that of Communist Russia.

Billions of dollars annually are fed to Cargill, who control most of America's grain and soybean trade. Their main 'competitor' ADM (Archer Daniels Midland), receives billions in subsidies to convert unwanted subsidised corn into ethanol to be burned with gasoline (see chapter 'Energy').

But the support of Congress-picked 'winners' doesn't stop at the US border. Billions of dollars a year go into the Market Promotion Programme and Export Enhancement Programmes to help Cargill and ADM compete against producers elsewhere in the world for contracts for wheat, corn and soybeans. Because Cargill and ADM benefit from subsidised prices, they get the contracts and local producers lose out. The mighty MacDonald's corporation and other burger companies expand their global empires on the back of sales of 99¢ hamburgers that would cost three times as much in the absence of corporate welfare. The entire world market for food has become grossly distorted. Small farmers worldwide go out of business as larger but less efficient producers in rich countries thrive on government handouts.

Economist Stephen Moore of the Cato Institute warns, "Every major US Cabinet department has become a conduit for government funding of private industry". They conservatively estimate that taxpayers pay about $75 billion year to support America's largest corporations. Ralph Nader, the Green Party candidate for President, estimates the total value as closer to $167 billion.

In a free society, the market selects ideas for investment. There is freedom from restriction, from coercion and from the use of force. When it is subverted, we don't just lose freedom of choice, we lose our personal freedom. 'Creative destruction' is the healthy mechanism whereby businesses with good ideas or products can challenge and replace existing industries. It may create losers, but it also creates winners who are keeping up with changes. If government takes one company's side against its smaller, newer competitors, then society as a whole is the loser.

America is not alone; the establishment of the EU with power vested in the European Commission means that corporate influence can be concentrated in one place, Brussels, rather than in national capitals all over the continent.

Two centuries of sugar subsidies show how easy it is to start out on the path to 'corporate welfare' and how fiendishly difficult it is to get off. In the Napoleonic Wars the British blockaded France's sugar supplies from Haiti and Louisiana in the hope that a sugar-starved French populace would rise up and overthrow Napoleon. But Napoleon, undaunted, set aside 80,000 acres for sugar beet growing. After Waterloo and the lifting of the blockade, cheaper sugar imports from the West Indies resumed, but the beet sugar industry, farmers and refinery operators, bribed, rioted and eventually forced a settlement that guaranteed them half of France's sugar market, at a permanent cost to the French taxpayer.

With expansion of the Common Market, this policy now pervades the EU. In each of eight countries, just one national company controls the entire national beet sugar quota: in Britain it is British Sugar, in France it is General Sucrière. The price of sugar in Europe is 3 times the world price, protected by tariffs and subsidies.

However, European sugar, grown with herbicides, eroding soil and costing so much to produce, appears 'cheaper' on the supermarket shelf.

Worse, subsidised exports mean that Europe's surplus goes to developing countries, displacing low-cost sugar producers such as Mozambique. So unsubsidised small producers suffer as their export markets are swallowed up by EU sugar. If trade is not fair and open, then everyone loses out – especially the poor.

In the USA things are no better. Every attempt by Congress to eliminate federal sugar price support is defeated by Senators or representatives who have received campaign contributions from the sugar producers. Sugar producers get 30 times more subsidy per acre than wheat producers. The cost to American consumers is $2 billion a year.

In Florida, the main sugar-producing state, alligators suffer endocrine disruption from pesticides used on sugar, leading, alarmingly, to inadequate penis development or even to sex change. 500,000 acres of the Everglades have been drained for sugar production that is blatantly uneconomic.

Taxpayers lose, Third World producers bound by WTO free trade agreements lose, confectionery industry workers in the US lose, too, as

confectionery manufacturers move to Canada or Mexico, where sugar sells at the world price. One small but powerful interest group harms fellow citizens, foreign producers and the environment in the scramble for government money.

🐚 Europe's sugar regime "preserves the interests of all the parties concerned. It was deliberately designed to this effect. It must be maintained". The European Sugar Manufacturers' Association

🐚 The sugar regime costs EU consumers and taxpayers $1.57bn every year.

🐚 "Europe's policies... are putting us at a disadvantage. They are rich and could give us a chance to live." Sugar can harvester, Mozambique.

The Great EU Sugar Scam
Oxfam Briefing Paper 27
www.oxfam.org.uk

Fair Trade

how much fairer?

We have been taught that free trade is a good thing. However, it is often deeply unfair, or, to use tougher language – unjust and exploitative.

Take chocolate as an example. It is a 'premium' food, associated with indulgence and luxury. However, it comes at a price that includes slavery, environmental degradation and poverty.

Imagine the cost of cocoa bean production as $900 per tonne. A small farmer who produces 10 tonnes per year and sells at $1,000 per tonne makes a profit of $100 per tonne or a total of $1,000. If the cocoa price were $1,100 then he would make $2,000 for his year's work. So, a small 10 per cent increase in the cocoa price doubles the farmer's profit. Yet traders insist on keeping prices as low as possible. It is this crucial difference that the Fairtrade organisation seeks to address by setting 'fair' prices.

In 1982, Felix Houphouet-Boigny, the President of the Ivory Coast, the world's largest producer of cocoa beans, boldly announced that cocoa prices were too low and they would not be selling that year's crop. The world markets went crazy and prices soared to $3,000. So, the Ivory Coast began to sell again and the price settled down. In the next few years USAID, Britain's Overseas Development Agency and their German, Dutch and Swiss counterparts all embarked on a global aid exercise to help small farmers in Honduras, Belize, Papua New Guinea, Solomon Islands, Malaysia and other non-African countries to 'reduce poverty' by planting cacao trees. By the early 1990s there was, therefore, global overcapacity in cacao and the price had settled down to less than $1,000. Now, whenever the price starts to rise, the huge spare capacity that has been created kicks into action and the price sags to a level that allows cocoa growers to survive – and nothing more. The world's leading

American, British, German, Dutch and Swiss chocolate manufacturers can sleep easy. There will be no more shocks from Africans with ideas above their station.

Should world prices be allowed to rise and farmers earn a decent profit, the impact on the price of chocolate bars would be minuscule. A $500 per tonne increase in cocoa prices on the cost of a large 100g bar of chocolate is two-thirds of one pence. Yet an extra $500 per tonne to a small producer can make a huge difference to a whole country's health system, education and future investment. So why not allow prices for cocoa to rise? If all a producer country's exports were based on principles of 'fair trade', the extra foreign exchange would help reduce their crippling interest burdens and support investment in economic development.

It was the ruthless logic of commodity markets, supported by unenlightened aid programmes that led to the development of a fair trade movement back in the 1990s. In Britain, the Fairtrade Foundation included Oxfam, Christian Aid and other charities. The international Fair Trade Labelling Organisation (FLO) was established to ensure that national standards of fair trade were observed in all 17 participating countries.

Fair trade's main focus is on pricing and social conditions:

Pricing – the price of production is set by experts, then a fair trade premium is added to ensure producers get a reasonable return. Payment is in advance, so producers get cash on delivery of goods. Long-term contracts offer security and sustainability to producer cooperatives.

Social – small producer cooperatives must be democratic. Plantation workers must have the right to form unions and have decent wages, and health and safety standards. Child labour is prohibited and there must be appropriate programmes for environmental sustainability. None of the 'dirty dozen' of the most dangerous agrichemicals are allowed.

Products that comply with Fairtrade Foundation's criteria are entitled to carry the Fairtrade Mark, an independent guarantee of good practice.

Fair trade commodities include coffee, tea, cocoa, bananas, mangoes, honey, orange juice and sugar. Because of the complexity of setting prices (tea, for example, comes in so many quality grades it is impossible to set one price that suits all) there is no universal fair trade standard. Fair trade cannot eliminate all risk or bring benefits to all, but it is a growing market. With even Starbucks selling Fairtrade Coffee and the MacDonald's subsidiary Aroma selling Green & Black's chocolate the tentacles of ethical trading are reaching deeper – even into the world of the multinationals.

Those lobbying for fair trade also seek structural changes to world trade. Cocoa imports to the EU are taxed at four per cent import duty because there are no European cocoa farmers that need protecting from competition. But if Third World producers themselves convert cocoa beans into cocoa powder and cocoa butter these products face import duty of 12 per cent. If they produce actual chocolate and export that to Europe then the import duty hurdle is raised to 34 per cent. This effectively prevents economic development.

The No Nonsense Guide to Fair Trade
David Ranson
Verso Books 2001
ISBN 1 859 84334 4

The USA

if we all ate the way they do

The average American is an obese American. National annual average consumption is 60 pounds of cakes and cookies, 23 gallons of ice cream, 7 pounds of potato crisps, 200 sticks of gum, 576 cans of fizzy drinks, 90 pounds of fat, 134 pounds of refined sugar. Those who eat still more of this nutritionally impoverished food are risking severe obesity

America may be in the lead, but it is not alone. The Fast Food industry, among others, is determined to get the rest of the world to catch up. Apart from the nutrition problems thereby created, there are huge 'resource' implications.

The amount of resources used by a person can be measured as an 'ecological footprint', a term relating to the area of land used to provide a person's (or nation's) requirement for resources and to absorb their waste.

It takes an estimated ecological footprint of 24 acres of land to sustain an American. A Canadian needs 17 acres and an Italian gets by on nine. As a nation, the US has an ecological footprint that exceeds all of North and South America. Europe is not far behind. By comparison, the ecological footprint of an Indian is 0.38 hectares, just under one acre.

It would take at least four Planet Earths to support the world's population on the American diet and lifestyle. Development that is based on increasing the income and consumption of the poorest 4.6 billion ignores the limits of the planet's resources. **Stopping wasteful over-consumption is a far more effective way to stop the mining of the earth's natural capital.** In America, the USDA Natural Resources Inventory calculates that 2.1 billion tons of soil were lost to wind and water erosion in 1992. As Mark Twain famously remarked: "The problem with land is they stopped making it some time ago".

The world has 1.3 billion hectares of cropland and 4.6 billion hectares of grazing land. The WWF estimates that we are already exceeding the carrying capacity of the earth by 30 per cent,

using up land and trees that are not being replaced, diminishing the stocks available for the increased world population of the future.

The waste from our over-consumption is a problem, too: CO_2, sewage and packaging materials all need to be reduced or recycled. Cutting back on excessive food consumption, particularly of meat, would help to bring resource-use into balance, while reducing the obesity that brings ill-health in its wake.

Societies that can reduce their ecological footprint may be the economic successes of the future. Those dependent on other nations' resources are in a precarious position. The US may have to resort to the violent capture of global assets in order to maintain a lifestyle that is built around motor vehicles and fast food. At the Earth Summit in Rio de Janeiro in 1992 George Bush Snr announced: "The American way of life is not negotiable". As far as the rest of the world is concerned, the future of life on Earth is not negotiable. Herein lie the seeds of future conflict.

As we look towards a sustainable future, counting the number of heads will not be as important as measuring the size of the feet.

The Soil Association in the UK estimates that a vegetarian family of 4 could be fed from 3 acres of land, or 3/4 acre (0.3 hectares) per person. A vegan family would eat well on even less without the need for livestock. These diets thus dramatically reduce a person's ecological footprint.

Our Ecological Footprint
Mathis Wackernagel, William Rees
New Society Publishers 1995
ISBN: 0 865 71312 X

Government

calling the shots

At times public interest is at odds with Government policy. So, how optimistic can we be that government policy can ever help rather than hinder progress towards healthier food and farming?

Few will deny that capitalism operating in free markets with fair competition brings economic benefit to all sectors of society and rewards innovation. But Adam Smith warned in Wealth of Nations, way back in 1776, that larger businesses would inevitably attempt to harness the power of Government to suppress smaller competitors to the detriment of overall prosperity. This seems to be what has happened to our food and farming.

In capitalism, wealth is measured as financial capital. That's how government does it too – it exists by taxing financial capital via income tax, corporation tax and sales taxes. But there are other forms of capital, 'social capital' and 'natural capital', that underpin financial prosperity and stability but are more difficult to value in a profit and loss statement.

Social capital is a village hall that has a different event on every evening and brings together the young, the old and the commuters. Voluntary organisations, cooperatives, clubs and societies build networks and support systems that lead to reduced crime, better health, care for the sick and elderly and greater trust between individuals. These efforts save Government money – in health, welfare and employment. **Natural capital** is the combined value of all the natural assets we enjoy: clean air, beautiful countryside and townscapes, fertile soil, unpolluted water.

When we protect Natural Capital we can spend less on restoring damaged environments, cleaning up pollution and dealing with its health consequences.

Government's job is to create a balance between the creation of financial capital and the maintenance and nurturing of social and natural capital. When the pressure on Government from financial interests outweighs that from social and natural interests then the economy as a whole is the loser. The question is how to gain that equality.

Take Britain's food and farming. The Department of Health and the Food Standards Agency exist to ensure that the food we eat is safe and of good quality. After the Foot and Mouth fiasco in 2001 the Ministry of Agriculture, Fisheries and Food was incorporated into a new Department for Environment, Food and Rural Affairs (DEFRA) to try to wrest policy from the grip of agribusiness. It appointed the Curry Commission, which recommended a move towards sustainable, entrepreneurial and multifunctional farming via an Organic Action Plan. After consultation with the RSPB, English Nature, the Soil Association and others, a plan was drawn up. However, President Chirac of France and Chancellor Schröder of Germany announced a backroom deal that ensured no real change in the Common Agricultural Policy's anti-environmental system of production subsidies until 2012.

This means that the EU will continue to encourage unsustainable production of unwanted animal feeds, oils, meat and dairy products and the continuing extinction of small farmers. In Brussels the agribusiness lobbyists must have quietly rejoiced at what amounts to victory over democratic choice, environmental health, the rural economy, animal welfare, organic farming, the developing world and human health.

Industry, as Adam Smith foresaw, lobbies constantly in government to bend policy in its direction. Lobbyists, often MPs or ex-civil servants, press for policies that favour their clients' interests, whether agribusiness, military equipment or pharmaceuticals. Small companies and industries have no such lobbying power, consumers even less. However, organisations such as the RSPB, Greenpeace, the Soil Association and the National Trust can sway policy towards the protection of natural and social capital. As these pressure groups become stronger, and make alliances at home and abroad, they can form an effective counterbalance to narrow industrial interests.

In *Uncommon Sense* Gregory Sams argues that, if insurance companies governed the world, there would be no nuclear power, no genetic engineering and no global warming. Simple – nobody can do business without insurance and insurance companies don't tolerate unfathomable or extreme risks. (It was pressure from insurance companies on Government that brought in mandatory seatbelts and other road safety measures.) But insurance companies don't run the world and nuclear power and genetic engineering are authorised by governments that exempt the participants from liability and the victims from compensation.

Government responds to market situations and organised political pressure. So does business. We can't do without Government or business, so we must make policy work to ensure the optimal balance between social, natural and financial capital. We can do this by actively supporting organisations that influence policy to make our food and farming better for us, for our children, farming families, rural communities and the natural environment. We can apply pressure on the food industry by buying safe and nutritious food. 'The hinge that squeaks loudest gets the most oil.' Squeaking loudly – through organisations, as individuals and through a free press – is the way to persuade Government to ensure that social and natural capital are not sacrificed for narrow, short-term financial gain.

"Freedom and liberty lose out by default because good people are not vigilant."
Archbishop Desmond Tutu

The Captive State
George Monbiot
Macmillan 2000
ISBN 0 333 90164 9

Join the NFU

putting your job on the line

Why do farmers have a union? It makes sense for farmworkers, but it is strange to see landowners, the epitome of independent property-owning enterprise, operating a union with powerful representation at the government ministry.

A union's success is usually measured by the number of jobs that it protects, the income it can negotiate and the degree to which it ensures safer working conditions.

The average age of a British farmer is now 59 – few young people can afford to farm or wish to do so; farm incomes have reached depressingly low levels; farmers are exposed to pesticides, particularly organophosphates that affect the nervous system. The result is that 6,000 farmers a year abandon farming – hardly a success.

Under subsidies on production farmers have become welfare – dependent employees of the state. But unlike single mums and unemployed miners, they have a powerful union and lobby fiercely at the highest governmental levels.

So what has the NFU achieved?

In November 2000 the first cases of BSE were found in France and Germany, a few years after cases in Britain were discovered. Sales of beef fell 40-50 per cent overnight. German and French farmers sought markets abroad where they could dump beef at low prices. UK producers faced the horrifying prospect of falling prices and demand. In February 2001, foot and mouth disease was found on a pig farm in Northumberland. Spurred by the NFU, the Ministry of Agriculture isolated affected farms, killing all animals. The Soil Association and others questioned the sanity of this mass slaughter and called for vaccination. The NFU shouted them down, claiming that consumers wouldn't eat vaccinated animals. Millions of cattle, sheep and pigs were slaughtered, often in horrifying conditions. The lack of British beef meant the market for beef stabilised as European supply and UK demand came into balance.

In the wake of the foot and mouth crisis, the government appointed Sir Donald Curry to chair a Food and Farming Policy Commission, to advise on the creation of a sustainable agricultural policy. On January 30, 2002 the commission published its report. It urged CAP reform and called for 'modulation' whereby $500 million out of the £3 billion given to British farmers each year be transferred from production support (i.e. subsidies per animal) to environmental funding.

PM Tony Blair welcomed the report. Ben Gill, NFU president, said "This supposedly big new idea of modulation is stupid, deceitful and immoral. The idea that you can take money out of my right pocket and put it into my left pocket and expect farmers to welcome it is incredibly naive. We will fight it strongly". However, reduced production subsidies would lead to a decline in use of fertilisers and pesticides, while the income to farmers would be the same, just paid into the 'left pocket'. The only sector that would suffer would be the agrichemical industry.

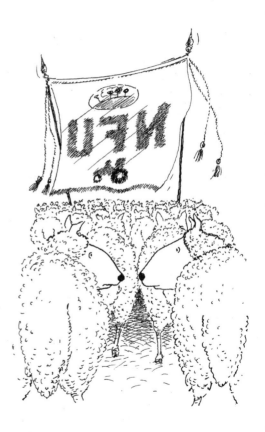

The NFU supports the introduction of GM crops and has invested millions of its own money in GM research. It also provides insurance through NFU Mutual insurance, yet the insurance policy contains the following disclaimer: "NFU Mutual will not indemnify the Insured in respect of any liability arising from the production, supply of or presence on the premises of any genetically modified crop". The irony is impressive.

Organophosphates cause nervous system damage to farmers and farmworkers. For safety reasons, the Government acted to phase out Carbaryl, an organophosphate used to thin apples chemically. The NFU reacted furiously at this attempt to protect its members from harm.

In its support for GM crops, dangerous pesticides, mass slaughter and the demise of small farms the NFU's role in agriculture seems to serve the interests of agribusiness more than it does the farmworker and the small and medium farmer.

- No-one is listening to the NFU anymore; it has no voice or political power, according to Simon Wetherall, the NFU's Somerset chairman. He has proposed that the union instead unlock the massive financial reserves held by its insurance arm to become involved in retailing and fight back against supermarkets.

- A September 2001 survey of over 500 independent and family farmers found that: 28% of farmers didn't feel that they had a representative organisation, 67% felt there was a need for a new body to represent independent and family farmers and 18% had dropped out of the NFU.

Pesticides

there's no escape

From planting to harvest, crops are attractive to seed-eating, sap-sucking, leaf-eating, root-nibbling pests. So we 'zap' them. Weeds grow vigorously when their surrounding crops are fed with artificial fertilisers. So we 'zap' them, too. Natural methods can protect crops, but poison is the cheapest solution. However, pesticidal poison is indiscriminate and its cheapness conceals an unpaid cost to society and the environment.

The World Health Organisation (WHO) estimates there are 500,000 pesticide-related poisonings per year including 5,000 accidental deaths. The US Environment Protection Agency reckon that between 10,000 and 20,000 cases of pesticide poisoning incidents occur among US agricultural workers each year.

But that's just the tip of the iceberg. Pesticides attack biodiversity, leading to loss of wildlife and the disappearance – forever – of species.

But pesticides have other talents. They can be:
Carcinogenic – causing cancer
Mutagenic – causing or increasing frequency of mutation
Teratogenic – damaging to an embryo or foetus
Fattening – when the liver cannot dispose of poisons they can be wrapped in fat and stored for later attention, i.e. as cellulite. (This is one reason why dieters often feel ill as shedding fat also entails pesticides re-entering the system.)
Endocrine-disruptors – some pesticide molecules are similar to human hormones such as oestrogen, so the body's hormone balance becomes confused and upset (see chapter 'Oestrogen').

Many of the worst pesticides, such as DDT insecticide and Atrazine herbicide, have been banned or restricted in the industrial world. Nonetheless, these chemicals continue to be used in poorer countries, giving rise to an unfortunate paradox. When a farmer in the tropics sprays his crops, some pesticides are carried up by evaporation into the rain clouds. Some rise into the stratosphere, where they are carried around the planet only to be re-released when the clouds pass over the colder polar regions, condense and fall as rain or snow. This is why Scandinavian countries have, ironically, such high levels of DDT in their environment and food, despite banning the chemicals in the 1960s. It is also responsible for childhood cancers and sexual deformity among the Inuit children of Canada because Arctic foods such as reindeer, cod and berry fruits have high levels of residues.

In Britain, all known sources of spring water still contain traces of the gender-changing, hormone-disruptor atrazine, despite its use being restricted in the early 1990s.

Other chemical use persists. A 2001 report by the Pesticides Residues Committee revealed levels of Dicofol (a DDT derivative) in strawberries at 10 times the maximum residue level (MRL). Dicofol use in Florida causes genital shrinkage in male alligators. It makes reproduction impossible. The report also showed higher pesticide residues in wholemeal (non-organic) bread than in white bread and that farmed salmon always contains significant levels of organochlorine pesticides (used to control sea lice).

Bran high-fibre cereals, lettuces, citrus fruit and apples also showed multiple residues at levels that raised concerns about the 'cocktail effect'. this means that three pesticides consumed together can have 100 times the damaging effect of each one eaten separately. The MRL for pesticides is set at 1/100th of the level at which tests have shown them to be harmful, so the accumulative effect of a cocktail of pesticides quickly negates individual safety margins set by regulators. Where crops are sprayed with as many as 36 different pesticides, some of them systemic, washing or peeling is useless. So, in an apparently healthy meal that includes salmon, brown bread, carrots, lettuce, apples and strawberries one could easily be consuming more than 100 pesticides. All this adds to the exposure to synthetic chemicals in bodycare and household products, plus the inhalation of airborne by-products of diesel and petrol engines. Who knows what the true cocktail effect is but it's worrying enough for The Food Standards Agency to have commissioned a

report from the Committee on Toxicity (COT) to find out more.

Another pesticide-related phenomenon is more apparent. 'Pesticide suicides' in India are estimated at 20,000 per annum. Farmers using pesticides find that pests develop resistance. So, more agrichemicals are needed and soil fertility declines. Eventually the whole process becomes unsustainable and the farmer is faced with leaving his land. Or he consumes enough pesticides himself to escape these problems – forever.

How can farmers reduce pesticide residues? Many pesticides are applied on a 'just-in-case' basis to prevent cosmetic damage by insects. For example, unripe apricots are sprayed to avoid insect damage that puts 'freckles' on the fruit. Hothouse plants such as lettuces, cucumbers and tomatoes are routinely sprayed against whitefly and red spider mite. But there are alternatives. Chemical-free methods include crop rotation, release of predator populations, traps, beetle banks and physical barriers. 'Companion planting' is a system where plants that repel certain pests are planted alongside those that don't. All these techniques are less than 100 per cent effective, so that you may find that the edge of a leaf has been nibbled or that there is an aphid lurking inside a lettuce leaf. However, the invisible risks from pesticides tip the balance, for many people, in favour of, for example, organic food.

If pesticides were stained bright blue so that residues showed up in food, who would buy blue fruit and veg?

- Biopesticides: Bacillus thuringiensis (Bt), a bacterium that kills insects, has been used successfully by organic farmers since the 1960s. It disappears three days after application and leaves no residues. However, its toxic secretion has now been engineered into patented biotech crops such as Bt maize. Insect resistance is already developing due to the continuous exposure of a permanently 'on' genetic modification and the persistent presence of Bt toxin in soil. An important tool of organic farming thus risks being lost.

- A Cuban biopesticide, Griselef, based on spores of *Bacillus sphericus*, is specific to mosquito species which feed on blood. It only needs spraying one to three times to wipe out a mosquito population, compared to 40-50 sprayings needed for Fenthion (an organopesticide that has replaced DDT). It is cheap and effective and, most important, causes no harm to humans, animals and other insects, just malaria-spreading mosquitoes.

- Most of Britain's parks, playing fields and golf courses use pesticides regularly. Few of them post notices or cordon off sprayed areas.

- 800 pesticides are used in the EU. In Britain alone 25,000 tonnes are sprayed on food crops every year. Pesticide contamination of drinking water already regularly exceeds safety limits in the UK, France and Benelux. In the UK £1 billion has been invested in equipment to remove it from drinking water, with an ongoing annual cost of £100 million. We, the water-consumers, pay the cost and the whole community pays the price.

Pesticide Action Network UK
www.pan-uk.org

Energy

it's exhausting

Fossil fuels are running out. The need for alternative sources of energy is urgent. 'Energy crops' are a hoped-for new market for agriculture and their story highlights much of what has gone wrong with modern agriculture.

In Germany, 'bio-diesel' blends use up surplus subsidised rapeseed oil by mixing it with diesel fuel for use by public service vehicles. In the US, petrol companies supply 'gasohol' which is a blend of 90 per cent petrol and 10 per cent ethanol – alcohol distilled from corn. Some have gone further and offer 'EP85' a blend of 85 per cent ethanol mixed with 15 per cent petrol. Although ethanol is more expensive, government tax breaks and allowances mean EP85 can be sold at the same price as petrol.

The National Corn Growers' Association boasts that over five per cent of US corn production in 2002 went to ethanol production. That's over three million acres of farmland devoted to reducing the use of fossil fuels. Or is it?

An acre of corn yields 328 gallons of ethanol. But that corn is grown using agricultural machinery, artificial fertilisers, pesticides and herbicides – all using fossil fuels. Converting it into a fermented mash and distilling it to produce ethanol uses yet more energy.

Cornell University estimates that it thus takes 1.7 gallons of fossil fuels to make one gallon of ethanol. The actual cost of corn ethanol is $1.74 per gallon, compared to $0.95 for petrol. Tax breaks and subsidies make it competitive – at a cost to the taxpayer of more than $1 billion per year. Even if the corn were free, and then converted to ethanol, it still wouldn't be competitive in the marketplace. (Ethanol could be made directly from fossil fuels for $0.95 per gallon, but the tax rebate only applies to ethanol made from corn or other biomass.)

It's not just fossil fuels that are wasted producing ethanol. Growing corn erodes soil 12 times faster than it can be reformed, leading to large-scale topsoil loss. Irrigated corn uses groundwater at a rate 25 times faster than the underground reservoirs are filling up and leads to salination. Topsoil loss and salination are why one per cent of the world's arable land is going out of production every year. All this waste and ethanol is sold as an 'ecological' fuel, because it reduces car pollution by five per cent. If every American drove an ethanol-powered vehicle the entire land area of the US would have to be given over to corn production for fuel.

So why is 'gasohol' being pushed so hard? As long as corn is subsidised more fertilisers, herbicides, GM seeds, pesticides and agricultural machinery can be sold. Rather than burning crop surpluses in the petrol tank, the land could be put into 'retirement', and fertility rebuilt. But there's nothing to show for that in the next quarter's

profit and loss accounts. Archer Daniels Midland (ADM) lobbies intensively to ensure the US Government keeps up the subsidies on ethanol. ADM produces more than 50 per cent of all ethanol used as fuel.

In the debate about genetic engineering the recurrent refrain of GM supporters is: "The world's population will soon reach 10 billion – without GM crops we won't be able to feed the world". Thirty one million acres of land are already out of production in the US under the Conservation Reserve Program; 3 million are devoted to producing corn ethanol. An estimated further 15 million acres produce corn that is converted expensively into corn syrup by ADM, with generous government subsidies. There's plenty of existing capacity to feed the world.

But there's a further argument for gasohol: it reduces America's dependency on fossil fuels from politically volatile areas such as the Middle East and Venezuela. "We don't need military expenditure to protect the corn fields of the Midwest," claim ethanol's proponents. As ethanol production is based on an increased need for fossil fuels the reverse is actually true.

Intensive agriculture takes 12 calories' worth of fossil fuels to produce one calorie of food. If oil prices rise the economics of agriculture change. With oil at $40 per barrel, intensive agriculture can no longer compete with low-input alternatives such as organic farming. The bio-fuels, too, would become even more expensive.

Fuel cells, solar power and other 'alternative' electricity generating systems will become more, rather than less, competitive as oil prices rise. However, the agribusiness and the oil lobbies continue to make them less-favoured options. The wasteful use of finite resources illustrates how the consumer/taxpayer's interest has been subverted by agribusiness's control of the political process.

Germany's 'Bio-diesel' is a blend of diesel oil with either rapeseed or soya oil, or animal fats such as lard or butter. The economics are, like those of petrol, dependent on subsidies to compensate for the cost differentials. It would be cheaper to buy the crops and throw them in the sea.

Food, Energy and Society
David Pimentel, Marcia Pimentel
Colorado University Press 1996
ISBN 0 870 81386 2

Organophosphates

the poison hierarchy

Before hormone usage the earliest growth promoters used in intensive animal production were organophosphates, where very low doses were enough to increase fat development. However, organophosphates, which are a 'broad-spectrum' class of insecticides, have known toxic effects on the nervous system. Large doses were used in the gas chambers at Auschwitz and were also tested for use as nerve gas in warfare.

Before considering organophosphates we have to look back at organochlorines. These were the first and least safe generation of pesticides that included DDT, Lindane, aldrin and dieldrin. All are persistent and accumulate in the food chain. Lindane, the last of the organochlorines still being used, was phased out in Europe in 2002 and is also banned in California, though permitted in the rest of the US. It is commonly used in developing countries, particularly on cocoa trees. It was, however, the clear association with increased risk of breast cancer that led, after much resistance from farmers and chemical companies, to the EU ban. The ban has encouraged farmers to look to other chemicals.

Organophosphates are claimed to be safer than the organochlorines, but evidence is emerging that they may be just as bad – in a different way. Their use during World War 2 should tell us something. As a nerve gas they slow the transmission of nerve impulses, causing nervous system and brain failure.

So why use it on cattle?

When organophosphates are consumed, they restrict the conversion of fats, held in reserve, back into glucose. Instead, the fat just accumulates. They damage nerves, weaken muscle fibres and reduce the desire to exercise – which helps produce tender, fatty meat. Organophosphates have finally been banned in agriculture as growth promoters in cattle, because of their toxic side effects.

In the UK, however, they are also used as a treatment on cattle for warble fly. Phosmet, a blend of a thalidomide compound and an organophosphate, is rubbed on the spines of cattle to get rid of warble fly larvae. From the spine, phosmet can penetrate to all parts of the cow's body, killing the infestation. Mark Purdey, a researcher in Somerset, argues that 'mad cow disease' could initiate from this practice. A foetal calf's head is positioned directly beneath the mother's spine, so could receive a direct dose of organophosphates at a crucial stage in the development of its nervous system.

Organophosphates are also still widely used on vegetable and fruit crops. In 2000, the British government found that 65 per cent of carrots sampled contained residues of the organophosphate Chlorfenvinphos.

Organophosphates are used in head lice lotions and creams for children. For years cosmetic and bodycare manufacturers have pooh-poohed the idea that the chemicals in their products could get into the bloodstream. That was before nicotine patches. It is now known that up to 60 per cent of what you put on your skin can enter your bloodstream. Unlike ingestion by mouth, where a substance has to pass through the defences of saliva, hydrochloric acid in the stomach and the protective flora of the digestive system, substances rubbed on the skin penetrate quickly and effectively. A study in 1997 by the Health & Safety Executive and Dr Vyvyan Howard of Liverpool University established that the organophosphate in head lice solutions could put children five times over government safety limits, and that repeated use may damage the nervous system. It is even thought that Creutzfeldt-Jakob disease could arise from head lice treatments. Alzheimer's disease symptoms closely mirror those of organophosphate poisoning.

Monsanto's Roundup herbicide may not be as immediately harmful as other organophosphates, but the intensive lobbying by Monsanto that led to the 200-fold increase in Maximum Residue Level for Roundup does mean some increased exposure. Roundup also contains 25 per cent polyacrylamide, which helps it stick evenly to plants. At high temperatures polyacrylamide breaks down into acrylamide, a strong carcinogen that has been found in potato crisps, crispbreads, chips and other foods cooked at high temperatures

Organophosphates are also used in sheep dips, flea treatments for pets, wood treatment, garden pesticides, and as additives in petrol, aviation fuel, lubricating oils and flame-retardant treatments.

Over-exposure to organophosphates produces what doctors call SLUD: Salivation, Lacrimation (tears), Urination, Defecation. This leads to paralysis, confusion, and convulsions ending in death by central respiratory failure. Lower level exposure has been connected with damage to the nervous system, depression, cardiac problems, and eye defects.

Organophosphates will probably, one day, be phased out as the evidence of their harm becomes overwhelming. Even the 'Five-A-Day' campaign to encourage people to eat more fruit and vegetables may suffer from consumer anxiety to avoid organophosphates. Cutting vegetables out of the diet, however, may be worse to health than consuming some residues. But if you regularly consume fruit and vegetables, it makes sense to avoid organophosphate residues. The obvious answer is to eat organic produce.

The Detox Diet
Paula Baillie-Hamilton
Michael Joseph 2002
ISBN 0 718 14545 3

Oestrogen

the feminising hormone

Most of us think of hormones, oestrogen for example, as natural substances that circulate in our bodies and affect behaviour and body cycles. Most of, however, don't know the full story.

The use of hormones in the production of meat really took off in the '60s. A synthetic version of the feminising hormone oestrogen, Diethylstilbestrol (DES), was heralded as a 'wonder drug' to beef feedlot farmers who inserted a hormone implant behind the ear of a heifer or steer to increase its weight – and their profit. DES also produced a fattier, more 'well-marbled' meat that made for juicier steaks. There were concerns about the risks to humans of consuming DES and farmers were told to remove the implant five days before slaughter to allow oestrogen levels in the meat to drop. Few farmers did so, as removal of the implant led to immediate weight, and profit, loss.

DES was also prescribed to women who had miscarriages to reduce the risk of miscarrying again. The supporting research, however, was flawed; miscarriages actually increased with DES, and it was banned when it was found to increase the risk of breast cancer too. Worse, it led to an even greater risk of breast cancer in the daughters of women who took DES because of excessive oestrogen during pregnancy. Worse still was the risk of breast cancer in their granddaughters. All the eggs a woman will ever produce are created in the foetal stage of her own development. So, the egg that produces the granddaughter was created by the grandmother. Effects can increase from generation to generation.

The discovery of the harmful effects of DES led to a call for a ban on its use as a growth promoter. This was fiercely resisted by farmers but by the 1980s both the US and EU had placed a ban. **A black market flourished among farmers** and illicit DES use continues, particularly in Southeast Asia, Latin America and Eastern Europe.

In the EU there is now, after years of pressure, an outright ban on the use of all hormones in meat production. In the US, however, other feminising hormones have been substituted for DES. To boost their effectiveness, they are combined with masculinising hormones – anabolic steroids – so that the animal goes through phases of fatty tissue development as the feminising hormones dominate, followed by rapid muscle growth as the anabolic steroids kick in, followed by more oestrogen-led fatty tissue development. The result is increased meat yield.

To protect such production methods, by the early 1990s over 20 States in the US had passed 'Agricultural Slander Acts' making it a criminal offence to criticise agricultural practices without indisputable scientific evidence. Fines can also be charged equal to the value of the estimated loss of sales suffered as a result of any 'slanders'. Without independent research and with the possibility that a court might side with scientists representing the hormone industry, there has

been an understandable reluctance to speak out. At the World Trade Organisation, the US went on to accuse the EU of putting up trade barriers by banning the import of hormone-enhanced American beef. The EU, anxious to protect its food exports to the US, but unwilling to compromise the health and sexuality of its citizens, made a concession: they agreed to allow the import of US beef as long as it was labelled as produced with growth hormones. European consumers could then make an informed choice. Not good enough, said the US; there's no risk so there should be no labelling. The WTO agreed, and in 2001 the EU was fined $120 million for fighting to keep hormones off our plates.

There are, however, other sources of hormones known as 'xen-oestrogens', or 'oestrogen-mimics'. Biologists in the 1970s discovered that male trout in the River Thames were changing sex. They assumed that women on the Pill were urinating out enough oestrogen compounds to be the cause. But the cause lay elsewhere – with 'oestrogen mimicry'.

The molecular structure of most herbicides is remarkably similar to that of the oestrogen molecule. When a herbicide molecule is consumed, it finds its way to the hormone receptors that are tailored to fit with oestrogen and its identity is mistaken. The body sometimes is confused into thinking that oestrogen levels are too high and stops the production of natural oestrogen, which can lead to **masculinisation in females.** At other times the oestrogen mimic activates femininity, with the possible effects of enlarged breasts in a male or female, or reduced testicle size in a male. Similarly, the presence of oestrogens and xenoestrogens increases the level of the male hormone testosterone. This breaks down into the chemical dihydrotestosterone, the main cause of prostate enlargement and cancer. There has been a greatly increased level of breast cancer in the late 20th century and testicular cancer is now the biggest cancer threat to 20-34 year-old males in the UK.

"It is conservatively estimated that most people have measurable quantities of between 300 and 500 chemicals in their bodies, which have been introduced to the planet within the last 50 years and would not have been present prior to that... It is generally agreed that foetal and infant life are the most susceptible periods for the action of hormone disrupting chemicals to have their maximum adverse effects".
Doctor Vyvyan Howard

In East Anglia, where intensive agriculture leaves high levels of herbicide spray drifting in the air and residues in the water supply, a woman's risk of developing breast cancer has reached 40%.

In Denmark the sperm count among organic farmers is double that of conventional farmers, possibly because of reduced exposure to herbicides and their oestrogenic effect.

My Year of Meat
Ruth L. Ozeki
Pan
ISBN: 0 330 36845 1

Genetically Modified Food

but can we eat it?

The patenting of discoveries about life is a new development. Hitherto, patenting has been restricted to innovation and invention. However, the existence of Genetically Modified Organisms (GMOs) is now a reality and for most people the primary concern is "Are GMOs and food containing them safe to eat?".

In 1993, 11 out of 17 scientists at the US Food and Drug Administration opposed the approval of the first GM tomato variety because of concerns about its safety after feeding trials. However, they were overruled by their bosses who were under great political pressure to grant approval. At the same time the FDA established a principle of 'substantial equivalence' which stated that GM foods no longer had to undergo safety testing since there was no significant difference between them and non-GM foods. It is this principle, which the US seeks to apply worldwide through WTO negotiations, that is at the heart of the debate about GM foods and safety. It is why the US opposes labelling of GM food – arguing that to give consumers a choice is to somehow imply that something is wrong with the GM option.

Although it is often claimed that GM foods are the most heavily tested in the history of the food industry, there have only ever been seven scientific feeding safety trials using GM food, five of which showed differences that were the cause of concern. Nor can we look to the manufacturers to take responsibility for safety.

The corporate attitude is summed up by the comments of Phil Angell, Monsanto's Director of Corporate Communications: "Monsanto should not have to vouchsafe the safety of biotech (GM) food. Our interest is in selling as much of it as possible. Assuring its safety is the FDA's job".

The feeding trials that have been carried out are not encouraging. Dr Arpad Puztai's research in 1998 showed that rats fed on GM potatoes developed intestinal lesions, or 'leaky gut' – similar to the results found with feeding trials using GM Flavr-Savr tomatoes in 1993. Ulcerative colitis, Crohn's disease, autism, malapsorption syndrome, food allergies and eczema are just a few of the diseases associated with leaky gut. Puztai was forced to resign but when the research was published, the Royal Society, Britain's national academy of science, called for further investigation. Unsurprisingly no scientist has dared take up the challenge and no biotech company has offered to fund such research.

In 2001 the British Medical Association report into GMOs claimed "insufficient evidence" to inform a decision on their safety.

In May 2002, 17 pig breeders in Iowa reported a sharp decline, up to 80 per cent, in the farrowing (conception) rate of breeding sows. All had one thing in common: they had only used their own farm-grown, genetically modified Bt maize in their pig feed. Iowa farmer Jerry Rosman commented: "We're working with a problem that no one has ever heard of before". The maize had unusually high levels of fusarium, a mould associated with fungal poisons known as

mycotoxins known to cause pseudo-pregnancy. This was a new and unknown mycotoxin that had emerged in reaction to the engineered toxin in the GM maize. The Iowa Farm Bureau recommended that farmers who breed their own pigs stop using GM corn. Humans who eat maize products – tortilla chips, corn flakes, corn bread and corn chips – were given no such warning.

In October 2000, after careful research into the matter, Munich RE and Swiss RE, the world's leading reinsurers, announced that they would not insure farmers or food processors for any liability arising from GM foods or farming. Since GM crops were now virtually uninsurable, the EU Commission and industry lobbyists pressured the European Parliament to put GM food producers beyond the normal laws of liability. (Much the same happened in the nuclear-power business; it was – and is – uninsurable. Governments have had to promise to cover the costs of accidents.)

Most of the research into GM crops is funded or performed by the companies that own the patents and have a financial interest in promoting GMO use. Bias often occurs in test results between independent researchers and those with a commercial interest. The biotech industry, for example, claims precision in the insertion of genes as a surety of GMO safety. Such claims, however, are undermined by the discovery that, while the human genome contains 30,000 genes, 250,000 different proteins are produced in the body. This means that some genes are multi-functional, with some functions that we don't yet understand. It isn't

surprising that unforeseen consequences of gene transfer have been found in plants – deformed cotton bolls, woody roots in soya beans, breeding problems in sows. Only extensive feeding trials can really assess the safety of GM foods.

Another argument put forward for the safety of GM foods is that Americans have been eating them since 1997 with no ill effects. However, food-related illnesses in the US are estimated to have doubled since 1997 and the accidental entry into the food chain, in 2001, of Aventis' modified Starlink maize led to many complaints of allergic reaction. In Ireland a rise in soya allergies has been reported since GM soya imports began and in the UK soya allergies have increased by 50 per cent since 1997. The use of GM soya must now be labelled.

GM food provides no real benefit to farmers. US farm subsidies have gone from $3 billion to $150 billion a year since GM crops were introduced. There are no nutritional benefits to GM food. The little safety testing there is indicates health risks. (Even the companies that sell GM seed are unhealthy. Calgene, who developed the Flavr-Savr tomato, went bankrupt and were bought by Monsanto, who ran out of money and were bought by Pharmacia Upjohn, who want to sell it off and concentrate on drugs, seeing no future in agricultural biotechnology.) They want a total monopoly and to deny consumers freedom of choice. Without that, the GM juggernaut may stop where it is. Meanwhile, GMOs are out there and questions about health risks remain unanswered.

- Plants such as maize, soybeans and oilseed rape are engineered to have herbicide resistance. This allows weedkiller, such as the herbicide Glufosinate, to be sprayed right up to harvest, greatly increasing the risk of residues in the final crop. Glufosinate is both a neurotoxin and a teratogen (causes embryo damage). Would these residues not seriously concern the bio-tech industry and our governments? Well, before the introduction of GM crops the biotech industry persuaded US and EU governments to increase the permitted residue of weedkiller in foods to 20,000 times the previous level.

- Soybeans with engineered brazil nut protein were never put on the market because of the risk of fatal anaphylactic shock in nut-allergic consumers of 'nut-free' products like soymilk.

- When GM rapeseed protein was fed to chickens their death rate doubled.

How to Avoid GM Food: Hundreds of Brands, Products and Ingredients to Avoid
Joanna Blythman
Fourth Estate 1999
ISBN: 1 841 15187 4

Fishing for Food

fishy business

Fish is good for us, but we are not good for fish. An abundant and valuable source of nutritious food is disappearing because of wasteful overfishing and pollution of the sea.

Fish is a source of essential fatty acids and is also rich in iodine, essential for the production of the thyroid hormone thyroxine, which regulates our energy levels. (See chapter 'Brain Food').

When the Grand Banks of Newfoundland were discovered in 1501 by Portuguese fishermen, they dropped baskets off the sides of their boats and lifted them out filled with cod. The ideal feeding and spawning conditions ensured a prolific supply of fish – until the late 1980s when cod stocks collapsed and the Canadian Government banned their fishing until levels recovered. The recovery has been far slower than expected. One reason for this is that cod don't reproduce until they are six years old and smaller fish fall victim to predators. The Canadian Government may have acted too late.

Deprived of fishing rights on the Grand Banks, European fishermen have sought fish elsewhere. The western coast of Africa provides rich fishing, and EU agreements with Mauretania and Senegal, burdened by debt and the need for foreign exchange, have opened up new fishing grounds inside their territorial waters. As the larger fish disappear the trawlers fish for smaller fish, often throwing back 80-90 per cent of the 'by-catch' that are not wanted or converting them to fish meal for sale to European fish farms. Senegalese and Mauretanian fishermen, who fish in small wooden boats intended for inshore use, have to go further out to sea in search of fish. Many never return. Others abandon fishing and migrate to Europe, where, ironically, they may find work on large trawlers fishing in their native waters. Fish and rice, a traditional dish and the source of 75 per cent of Senegalese protein intake, has become a scarce luxury.

How safe is fish?

Persistent organic pollutants such as dioxin and polychlorinated biphenyls (PCBs) from industrial waste, ship paints, insulation and pesticides, build up in fish, particularly in oily fish and in fish livers. The manufacturers of fish oil capsules have found it difficult to keep within maximum residue level limits. Indeed cod liver oil can have high levels of dioxins. The Irish Sea is estimated to contain a quarter of a tonne of plutonium as well as other nuclear wastes. These and other pollutants find their way up the food chain to fish. As a result it may be best to eat fish only twice a week, enough to obtain the nutritional benefits without accumulating too many pollutants.

What about farming fish?

Aquaculture, or fish farming, is held out as the answer to the decline in wild fish stocks. However, it has problems of its own. A farmed salmon that escapes, may breed with a wild salmon, destroying the latter's genetic integrity. Antibiotics are used routinely to suppress disease and alleviate stress. Ivermectin, for example, is added to fish-feed to control sea lice, and organophosphates are poured over the salmon cages. The Pesticides Residue Committee finds these residues in all farmed salmon.

Sea lice infestations are considered responsible for the collapse of sea trout populations in the area of salmon farms. When wild salmon swim

out to sea past salmon farms they become so infested with sea lice that they are often too weak to reach their feeding grounds in Iceland and Greenland. If they do get there they find that the herring they would normally feed on have been netted to feed farmed salmon.

It takes 3-5 kilograms of wild fish to make enough feed to produce one kilogram of farmed salmon.

Farmed salmon has higher fat content, but a lower content of the DHA and EPA essential fatty acids that make it nutritious. In blind taste-tests farmed salmon loses every time. The seabed beneath salmon cages takes years to recover from the pollution of excreta, drugs and pesticides used in the cages.

Fish farmers say the answer to these problems is genetic engineering – salmon that grow to seven or eight times normal size at a more rapid rate. All the problems of disease, escapes and pollution would be magnified. Brilliant!

The problem isn't confined to salmon. Sand eels, a vital component of a cod's diets in spring and early summer, are vacuumed up by Danish trawlers and then converted into fish oil and fish meal, contributing to the fall in North Sea cod stocks.

There are alternatives to fish that provide comparable nutrients, including seaweed for iodine, and hemp, flax seeds and oils for essential fatty acids. However, the sea is a hugely productive resource that could provide us with an endless supply of food if only we were to manage it in a sustainable manner.

The Marine Stewardship Council certifies fish that is produced in a sustainable fashion – Thames herring for example.
The Soil Association certifies the St. Helena fishery in the South Atlantic. It is unpolluted, operated by local fishermen and does not deplete fish stocks.

Marine Stewardship Council
www.msc.org

Seafood Watch
www.mbayaq.org/cr/seafoodwatch.asp

Animal Welfare

lives at stake

Most people love animals, but when it comes to eating them, people have ways of resolving the inner conflict between kind feelings for them and an appetite for their flesh, milk or eggs. Animal husbandry, the breeding and rearing of stock animals, has a tradition as long as arable agriculture. Issues of welfare and cruelty have only become a concern in the past few decades.

Before the introduction of antibiotics and other prophylactic drugs into agriculture, intensification just wasn't possible. If a farmer squeezed too much milk out of a cow, packed too many pigs in a shed or too many chickens in a cage the animals would die of disease. Farmers knew the limits and those limits corresponded with a reasonable existence for the animals.

The economic advantages of intensification are considerable: reduced expenditure on housing as more animals fit into a smaller space, reduced expenditure on labour and, because the animals don't use up energy walking around, better conversion of feed into meat. The impact on animal behaviour is inevitable – they attack each other in the hateful states that intensive habitation induces. To avoid this, chickens are debeaked, piglets have their tails chopped off, turkeys have their toes clipped and cattle have their horns removed. Dairy cattle are bred to produce so much milk that their bones crumble after a year or two. Mastitis is common, as are metabolic disorders arising from a diet of concentrated feeds.

As slaughterhouses become larger and able to process more animals per hour, issues of animal welfare in transport arise. Animals have longer distances to travel to their ultimate fate. 80,000 pigs die in the US every year in transport. Once at the abattoir, pigs that are not successfully stunned are boiled alive in scalding-tanks. Cattle that are improperly stunned bleed to death as their insides fall to the floor.

People suffer, too. Slaughterhouse workers have high accident rates, low pay and psychological disorders.

Consumers are generally disgusted by cruelty to animals, but many are reluctant to pay the cost for meat produced to higher welfare standards. Periodic exposés lead only to a temporary drop in meat consumption. However, revulsion at farm animal cruelty is a major factor in the growth of vegetarianism. Freedom Foods and organic meat do provide an alternative.

Farmers don't voluntary engage in cruel practice, though they become hardened to suffering after repeated exposure. Faced with the choice between bankruptcy or cruelty to animals, few choose losing the farm. As long as their customers buy only what is cheapest, they will only produce what they can sell profitably.

The EU has introduced welfare standards that improve the worst aspects of animal rearing, including the ending of caging chickens by 2012.

But the US is going in the opposite direction. Many states have amended their laws to exclude farm animals from anti-cruelty legislation. Consumer concern, however, can and does motivate fast-food companies to act. MacDonald's, under pressure from PETA (People for Ethical Treatment of Animals) now buys eggs from suppliers who use larger cages and reject debeaking. They have also told suppliers that by 2005 their pork supplied should be reared without hormones or antibiotics. This will force less cruel and intensive practices on farmers and lead to improved animal health.

The availability of healthier meat may also help to retard the growth of our own health problems that arise from fatty, diseased, drugged and hormone-implanted meat. Animals' suffering is, ironically, our suffering.

The Food Revolution
John Robbins
Conarie Press 2001
ISBN: 1 573 24702 2

Functional Food

pharming the food supply

Functional foods burst onto the market back in March 2000 with mass media advertising and impressive heath claims. Novartis, a leading pharmaceutical company, launched the 'Aviva' range stating: "Substantial benefits in heart, digestive and bone health can all be achieved by an appropriate choice of diet. Eating a balanced diet and taking regular exercise greatly assist our health and the likelihood of well-being in later years. However, the pace and demands of modern living can compromise the feasibility of an optimal lifestyle, reducing the positive contribution that diet and exercise can make".

In a nutshell, functional foods compensate for the junk food diet, lack of exercise and stress of modern life. In most cases they include healthy ingredients with proven health benefits, but they are usually mixed with the very same foods that cause ill-health.

Functional food developed from the involvement of the pharmaceutical industry in food production. Agriculture represents one part of their income; food processing another. Out of this melding of agriculture and medicine, functional foods were created to build on the concept of fortified food. A food that has been refined needs to have back some of the nutrients that went missing in the process, or deficiency diseases are a risk. Adding calcium and B vitamins to white bread is a common example. We now know that, as well as vitamins and minerals, processing also discards important nutrients such as – wait for it – fructo-oligosaccharides, anthyocyanins, betacarotene and phenolic compounds. The adding back of a few nutrients ('added value') allows the manufacturer to prescribe a single set of additives while ignoring the wide range of individual nutritional needs.

Diet and nutrition are replacing drugs and surgery as the foundation of a healthy life for many people. The trend towards healthy eating is the foundation of the organic and natural products industry. Meanwhile, the pharmaceutical industry has thrived by selling drugs to alleviate the symptoms of disease, much of which is caused by poor diet. They've lobbied vigorously to suppress competition from natural products such as herbs and nutritional supplements. With functional food they hope to hitch a ride on the trend towards healthy diet and preventive medicine.

The basic premise of functional food is always the same. Take a poor-quality food, add a few 'magic bullets' and sell it as a cure for chronic health problems. The benefits are questionable.

Aviva, for example, had three categories of product: Heart Benefits, Digestive Benefits and Bone Benefits:

- Oat bran and Vitamins C & E are added to their Heart Benefits foods to help reduce cholesterol. Oddly, they also contain 20 per cent hydrogenated fat and 40 per cent sugar, which help increase harmful cholesterol.
- Bone Benefits bars contains magnesium and calcium to help replace bone but again, a high level of sugar and hydrogenated fat undermines overall health.
- Digestive Benefits bars contain 20 per cent fructo-oligosaccharides (FOS). This is a 'prebiotic' that helps friendly 'probiotic' intestinal bacteria. However, they also contain 40 per cent white sugar, which is what upsets healthful bacteria levels in the first place.

These products rely on the benefits of one ingredient in isolation and ignore powerful negative co-factors such as sugar and hydrogenated fats.

So, how successful are functional foods?
"Out of 1,100 products launched in the nutraceuticals industry last year, only 42 reached $1 million in sales," revealed David Weinberg of Lerner Health Products back in March 2000. That's less than a four per cent survival rate.

The confectionery industry is one of the last hopes for functional food. The June 2002 *Candy Industry* magazine comments: "Confectionery manufacturers can take nutritional ingredients and put them in a convenient form that looks and tastes better than a couple of pills." Sugar,

associated with heart, bone and digestive disease, is now seen as the most effective vehicle for delivering isolated healthy ingredients.

The Aviva range was withdrawn after failing to achieve expected sales in the UK, though it is still available via doctors in the US and UK.

Truly 'functional' products such as yoghurt, wholewheat bread and oat porridge have been doing their good work for millennia. Adding a few nutritionally valuable ingredients to a junk food diet is a 'sticking plaster' approach that misses the 'aware' consumer and is of little interest to the junk-food lover. For some, the presence of a few vitamins or nutrients might compensate for the guilt felt at eating sugary snacks instead of a proper meal, but a proper understanding of a healthy diet is too complex and specific to the individual to be packaged in a snack bar, fortified drink or enriched biscuit.

- Genetic engineering offers the promise of being able to insert desirable nutritional characteristics into foods, but can the market for such products, judging by the market problems of functional foods, justify the development cost?

- The answer to most of our nutritional problems stares us in the face: eat good, natural food.

The Functional Foods Revolution
Michael Heasman, Julian Mellentin
Earthscan 2001
ISBN: 1 853 88687 7

Antibiotics

the impact on human health

The introduction of penicillin in 1935 heralded a new era in medicine: the development of antibiotics. Diseases which had formerly been incurable could be treated effectively with these new 'wonder drugs'. Many millions of lives were to be saved. Over time, however, resistance to antibiotics emerged and more and more antibiotics ceased to be effective. Perhaps this was inevitable, but the development of resistance has been accelerated by a number of factors:

- Hospital use of antibiotics to cut cleaning and labour costs in place of expensive sterilisation and hygiene methods
- Unnecessary prescriptions by doctors, often for viral conditions for which they are ineffective, such as the common cold
- Routine addition of antibiotics to animal feeds as growth promoters. By killing off an animal's normal digestive flora antibiotics allow more of the animal's food intake to be converted into meat. The natural resistance to disease is lost; the antibiotics replace the natural immune function.

More than 70 per cent of all antibiotics used worldwide are used in agriculture. Many of these are identical or very similar to those used in human medicine. When bacteria develop resistance to an antibiotic they can 'teach' this resistance to other bacteria.

Staphylococcus aureus (MRSA), a common hospital infection, used to be treated by vancomycin until a new variant emerged. The excessive use of avoparcin, a vancomycin-like antibiotic, is probably the cause. Avoparcin was banned in 1997, but by then the resistance had been transferred. In Japan some hospitals have been closed and sealed shut in an attempt to contain the resistant bacteria. In the UK it is a common, and serious, problem in hospitals.

Genetic engineering to produce resistance also presents a further risk. Despite its proponents' claims of precision, the insertion of genes is highly random. If a GM product is fed to an animal the resistant DNA can be transferred to bacteria in that animal's gut, rendering antibiotics used as medicine useless. Antibiotic-resistant genetic material may no longer be used in genetic engineering, but it is still the base of most 'first generation' genetically engineered animal feed crops.

Most antibiotics evolved in soil where their function is to help maintain the balance of life in the 'soil food web'. Antibiotic residues in manure and in slurry runoff encourage the development of antibiotic resistant bacteria in soil and in the water supply, further increasing the risk of transferred resistance. Any antibiotic residues that find their way into the food chain upset the natural balance of our intestinal flora and the 'digestive food web'.

There are a number of regularly consumed foods that are produced with the use of antibiotics. They include:

Chicken – battery chickens for meat are fed growth-promoting antibiotics throughout their lives. Free-range chickens are antibiotic-free.

Turkey – ionophores, a group of drugs known to have neurotoxic effects on animals at low levels, are fed daily to prevent parasite infection. One in four turkeys from a flock in East Anglia didn't make it to the vital Christmas 2001 date because of poisoning from ionophores.

Eggs – though laying hens are not fed antibiotics as growth promoters, they are fed antibiotics to control parasitic diseases that are common in intensive egg-production systems. Residues have been found in eggs.

Beef – feedlot beef cattle, reared on grain, are regularly fed growth-promoting antibiotics. Grass fed cattle are not.

Pork – pig rearing depends heavily on antibiotics. Piglets that are weaned prematurely develop pneumonia easily and are treated with antibiotics. Up to ten different antibiotics are used in pork production, for disease prevention and growth promotion.

Milk – when a milking cow goes dry a few months before giving birth to a calf, a tube of antibiotics is inserted into the chambers of her udder to prevent mastitis. This infuses the calf's first milk intake.

Fish – antibiotics in fish farming are commonplace and spread into the environment, affecting wild fish and shellfish.

The chicken industry is already walking a tightrope, alternating drugs to an agreed rotation, hoping to extend the effectiveness of antibiotics. Nonetheless there have been failures. One large chicken factory in Wales has been closed down and the entire building disinfected in order to eliminate resistant strains of disease. Antibiotics are never routinely used on any animals under organic farming systems. When an organically reared animal is ill, antibiotics may be used as a last resort. If this happens, the animal cannot be sold as meat, nor its milk or eggs be sold as 'organic' until after a withdrawal period.

In Sweden and Denmark, with government funding assistance, farming standards have changed to avoid the need for antibiotics. Other countries need to make changes, too. It is little help imposing quality standards on domestic producers without controls on imports, as they merely import the superbug problem.

The 1970s saw the last big breakthrough in antibiotic development. Now a new antibiotic is being trialed – Ziracin – with high hopes for its ability to control hospital 'superbugs'. Yet even as Ziracin is being tested, an almost identical drug, Avilamycin, is being introduced as a growth promoter to replace the four other antibiotics that have been banned in chicken production by an increasingly worried British government. The risk of resistance developing is high.

With no new antibiotics in the pipeline, drug companies need to increase sales of existing ones. Advertising in publications such as Farmers Weekly encourages excessive antibiotic use, helping to ensure that the consumer gets cheap chicken in the short run but less effective health care in the long run.

In the Northeast US in April 2002 there was an outbreak of Salmonella Newport contracted from contaminated hamburger beef. Medical

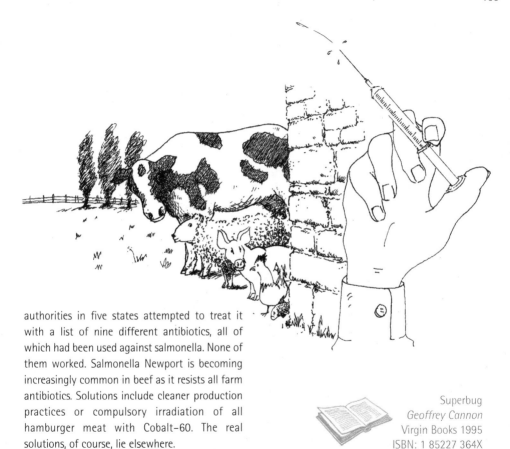

authorities in five states attempted to treat it
with a list of nine different antibiotics, all of
which had been used against salmonella. None of
them worked. Salmonella Newport is becoming
increasingly common in beef as it resists all farm
antibiotics. Solutions include cleaner production
practices or compulsory irradiation of all
hamburger meat with Cobalt-60. The real
solutions, of course, lie elsewhere.

Superbug
Geoffrey Cannon
Virgin Books 1995
ISBN: 1 85227 364X

Additives

hidden and blatant

'Added value' is the term that processors use to describe the profit from the transformation of food stuffs into a ready-to-eat form. Time is money, so the value of processing represents the saving of the customer's time. Nutritional value, however, can often be lost.

The adulteration of food has a long and inglorious history. Medieval bakers were marched in shackles through the streets, pelted with rotten fruit and abuse, for the addition of finely ground chalk and sawdust to add whiteness and weight to bread. Water was added to milk or wine, pig's blood gave colour to stale fish. Brick dust was added to cocoa, red lead gave the deep orange colour to Gloucester cheeses, used tea leaves were dyed with black lead.

A modern processor can make a profit in two ways: by improving ingredients in a way that is difficult for a cook at home, or by diluting the character of the food – by adding ingredients that cost less than the food itself. The cheapest are air and water, the processor's favourites. But they come with problems:

- **loss of flavour**
- **loss of colour**
- **loss of texture**
- **poor appearance**
- **risk of microbial attack and oxidation**

So, artificial flavourings, colourings, bulking agents and preservatives help further to mask the loss of quality. The Sale of Food and Drugs Acts in 1875 made it an offence to sell food which was not 'of the nature, substance or quality of the article demanded'. In 1978, however, 'E' numbers were introduced to save manufacturers the trouble of naming all the additives, but consumers mistrusted these lists. *E for Additives* became a best-selling book, detailing the identity of each E number and its known side effects.

Why the concern?
Additives are a worry because, among other things, they **affect learning ability in children, cause hyperactivity and can be hormone disruptors, carcinogens and mutagens.**

Legislation on food labelling might appear to be the answer. However, it enables processors to avoid the issue because there are some additives that don't have to be listed on product labels.

The worst example is 'compound ingredients'. If the individual ingredients that make up a compound ingredient are less than 25 per cent by weight of the product, they do not need to be listed. So, a jam-filled biscuit might list 'raspberry jam' but not mention what the jam itself contains, which might include preservatives, artificial flavourings, colourings and other undesirable ingredients. Thus manufacturers can 'remove' preservatives from their ingredient lists by putting them into a compound ingredient such as 'natural flavouring'. This way they avoid declaring preservatives at all and the consumer assumes there are none.

There have been proposals to limit this abuse but only by lowering the 25 per cent ceiling to five per cent. But, as preservatives, artificial colourings and flavourings usually make up less than one per cent of the product there is little benefit in such a change. People with allergies are sensitive to very small quantities of the allergens; they need to identify all ingredients. The label 'may contain nuts' is the manufacturer's failsafe put on a product that has been made in a factory that handles nuts. The label 'may contain diphenyl' (a fungicide used to coat citrus fruits) on a lemon or in lemonade would be less acceptable.

Reading the label
'Natural' flavourings are not natural. They have the same chemical formula as the ingredient found in nature, but are made from petro-chemicals. They are more durable than the natural flavours to which they are 'identical' and cannot be detected by analysis. 'Natural flavour' is derived from a natural source.

'Flavouring' often indicates the presence of monosodium glutamate or hydrolysed vegetable protein. (See chapter 'Tastes Familiar') Artificial flavours compensate for the lack of taste in poor-quality products, particularly factory-farmed meat. Cured smoked bacon is expensive to produce; smoke flavouring and artificial colouring are cheaper. Tasteless broiler chicken is tumbled in a liquid solution that contains hydrolysed beef or pork extracts to infuse it with flavour and increase its weight by up to 30 per cent. The addition of water need not be declared unless it exceeds statutory permitted levels (10 per cent of the weight of the meat).

Colourings are a particularly sensitive subject. Tartrazine, a popular yellow colour, causes hyperactive behaviour and violence in children. To avoid listing it as an additive it can be placed under the root system of orange trees to ensure the resultant orange juice is the right colour and can still be labelled '100% pure'.

Hydrogenated fat, thanks to its plastic-like hardness, gives structure and texture to biscuits and bread. More air and water can be added without the end product collapsing or crumbling.

Preservatives are particularly important when water has been added to a product. Many foods have a natural stability which helps them to resist deterioration and microbial attack. However, if a product has been injected with water this resistance is lost and preservatives are needed to protect it from the development of pathogens. Preservatives, like antibiotics, randomly kill bacteria and so affect the digestive flora of the gut. (See chapter 'The Digestive System')

The 25 per cent compound ingredient rule and the proposed five per cent rule will only affect certain foods. Wine and beer contain a wide variety of adulterants, colourings, flavours, preservatives and processing aids that are excluded from labelling requirements. Confectionery and chocolate products sold loose also escape labelling law.

Organic food regulations only allow a handful of permitted food additives and those are all of natural origin, such as soy lecithin or citric acid. Organic labels must declare all ingredients, regardless of percentage content.

A consumer cannot make an informed choice about food unless the information is available on packaging. This may present some difficulties to packaging designer but how else are we to trust our food?

'Golden Fields' white bread sold in New York contains '20 per cent fibre from natural forest sources'; they've put the sawdust back in bread. Calcium carbonate (chalk) is added to white bread to boost its calcium content. Medieval bakers would be amused to discover that their adulterants are now marketed as healthy additives.

A popular 19th-century story told of the customer who asked for a discount on sausages as he'd been a loyal customer for seven years. "Seven years!" exclaimed the butcher, "and you're still alive?"

E for Additives
Maurice Hanssen, Jill Marsden
HarperCollins 1987
ISBN: 0 722 51562 6

Wholegrains

the perfect food

Every great civilisation of history has been founded on wholegrains. Civilisations evolved when a farmer managed to produce enough wholegrains to feed himself, his family and his community. In turn, the people who asserted control over the food supply – warriors, priests and princes – prospered. Nutritionally, wholegrains provided such a sound dietary foundation that the vagaries of the rest of the diet did not undermine overall health.

A recommended modern diet can be represented by the 'Food Pyramid', with cereal foods as the basis of a healthy diet. [see charts on following page] The arguments for such a recommendation are strong.

Wholegrains protect against cancer, (particularly stomach and colon cancer), and reduce the risk of coronary heart disease, diabetes and hypertension – all this because of their high content of dietary fibre, starch, oligosaccharides, trace minerals, vitamins, antioxidants and phytoestrogens.

Wholegrains include wheat, rice, maize (corn), oats, rye, barley, sorghum and millet. Wholewheat and brown rice each represent 31 per cent of the world's grain production. However, 21 per cent is milled white rice. The other 10 per cent – rice bran and germ – goes for animal feed. Each year nearly 200 billion kilos of highly nutritious rice bran and germ and a further 100 billion kilos of wheat germ and bran are refined out of the human food chain. This represents 300 kilograms per annum of nutritious food for each of the 1 billion people on the planet who go to bed hungry.

A whole cereal grain contains three main parts: the endosperm, germ and bran. Endosperm is mostly carbohydrate, with up to 10 per cent protein. The germ is rich in nutrients including vitamins, minerals and oils. The bran is the outer casing and is also known as 'dietary fibre'.

Until recent times, most grains were ground on millstones. To remove some of the bran and germ it was 'bolted' – shaken through a coarse material – to give fine whiteish flour. This was an expensive process, so white bread was a luxury reserved for the wealthy.

The first roller mills appeared in the 1880s. Now the bran and the germ could be removed separately to leave white flour. White bread became available to the masses. The nutritious germ and bran were sold for animal feed or to early health-food suppliers.

When industrial rice mills were introduced into Asia, and white rice became easily available, outbreaks of beri-beri were noted. This is a Vitamin B1-deficiency disease that leads to numbness, confusion and mental instability. Experiments in the Kuala Lumpur Lunatic Asylum in Malaya in 1907 published in *The Lancet* showed that substituting brown rice for white cured mental illness. As a reaction 'parboiled' rice is now eaten widely where rice is a staple. In this process, wholegrain 'paddy' rice is steeped in hot water long enough for the B vitamins in the rice bran to soak into the grain and so help prevent beri-beri.

In the West, the main result of eating more white bread was constipation and a burgeoning market for laxatives. But millers were happy because white flour meant fewer pest problems – insects cannot survive or reproduce on a diet of white flour. By the 1940s, however, it was clear that white bread was nutritionally inadequate and 'fortification', the adding back of missing nutrients, became mandatory for white flour.

What are the benefits of Wholegrains?

All grains contain a balance of carbohydrate and protein that corresponds closely to the balance needed in our diet. But wholegrains have more.

Fermentable Carbohydrates

Wholegrains contain high levels of 'fermentable carbohydrate', including dietary fibre and oligosaccharides. These keep the contents of the intestine moving and gently scour any accumulations of fibre-free sticky foods such as cheese, beef or white flour. This hurries food

Fats, oils & sweets
USE SPARINGLY

Milk, yogurt, cheese
2-3 SERVINGS

Meat, poultry, fish, dry beans, eggs, nuts
2-3 SERVINGS

Vegetables
3-5 SERVINGS

Fruit
2-4 SERVINGS

Bread, cereal, rice, pasta
6-11 SERVINGS

Recommended daily servings

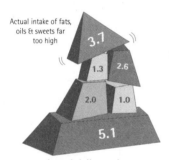

Actual intake of fats, oils & sweets far too high

3.7

1.3　　2.6

2.0　　1.0

5.1

Actual daily servings

through the digestive system, ensuring that toxins are excreted before they can be reabsorbed. These carbohydrates aren't digested in the small intestine but are fermented in the colon by intestinal flora to produce short chain fatty acids. The best known of these is butyrate, important in maintaining the health of the cells in the colon, decreasing the risk of cancer.

Blood Sugar Levels

The dietary fibre of wholegrains also slows the rate of digestion and absorption of carbohydrates. This helps moderate blood sugar levels, reducing the risk of obesity and diabetes.

Prebiotics

These are the non-digestible carbohydrates, or 'fructo-oligosaccharides (FOS), that nourish the 'friendly' intestinal flora.

Wholegrains are rich in vitamins, trace minerals and a variety of phytonutrients that protect against cancer and ageing. They are an excellent source of vitamin E and selenium.

What's more, wholegrains, properly prepared, taste delicious and their bulk discourages overeating because they give a sense of fullness. They are the most economic use of the Earth's food-producing resources and represent a sustainable way of maintaining health.

Hope's Edge: The Next Diet for a Small Planet
Frances Moore Lappé, Anna Lappé
Jeremy P. Tarcher 2002
ISBN: 1 585 42149 9

Nutrition and Food Quality

getting what we need

What makes food good for you? Is it just the 'primary metabolites' such as vitamins, minerals, carbohydrates, fat and protein content? The discovery of vitamin and mineral deficiency-related diseases was a major breakthrough in nutrition studies and led to the fortification of refined foods such as white bread and breakfast cereals. Or is there more to food than A, B and C?

Since 1940, McCance and Widdowson's *Composition of Foods*, has had to be regularly updated. In that time key minerals in food have decreased by 40 per cent, reflecting the decline in mineral content of soil since the widespread use of agrichemicals began. Plants grown with agrichemicals do not develop the same healthy defences as plants grown organically because pesticides and artificial fertilisers replace functions normally those of the plant. A healthy plant has its own immune system and secretes substances that help it deal with the stress of disease and insect attack. These are the micronutrients, many of which – flavonoids and anthocyanins for example – are antioxidants. They have only recently been recognised as important in neutralising the 'free radicals' in food that induce cancer and other diseases. Eating these healthy plants can make an important contribution to the health of an animal or human being. Flavonoids help regulate our hormones and cell growth. Anthocyanins help eye function and the nervous system. Terpenes such as carotenoids prevent breast and prostate cancers. Sulphur-containing

glucosinolates and allicins prevent cancer, help heavy metal removal and protect the heart. The *Composition of Foods* doesn't have measurements of these micronutrients dating back 50 years. It is, however, now known that when plants get high levels of artificial nitrogen fertiliser and are sprayed with pesticides and fungicides they produce much lower levels, not just of the main vitamins and minerals, but of these key nutritive elements as well.

Thus, the question as to whether organic carrots have higher levels of vitamin A or not is of interest because it indicates whether other important nutrients are also present. We are looking at the immune system of the carrot.

What about the essential vitality of food? We instinctively know that the healthier food is, the more likely it is to do us good. Given the choice between a sick, crippled chicken with missing feathers or a fit one with glossy plumage, we go for the healthy bird that exhibits all the signs of natural vitality. It takes little imagination to conclude that if these plants and animals thrive on an organic system, the same must be true for human beings too.

Measuring the vitality of food is an elusive goal. Bio-crystallisation methods look at patterns of crystallisation of copper compounds when exposed to the juice of plants. A distinct pattern emerges, with tighter and more coherent crystals being typical of organic plants. But interpretation and explanation remain at an early stage.

Because of the economic importance of livestock, many advances in nutritional understanding come from research into animal health rather than human health. This may sound strange, but a sick animal is a financial loss to a farmer whereas a sick human represents income opportunities for the medical industry. Animal feeds are carefully mixed to ensure that deficiencies are minimised. Feeding trials have shown that animals decline in health over generations if fed on foods grown with fertilisers and pesticides. Reproductive and sperm motility problems occur. Many breeders choose organically grown feed to maintain desirable genetic traits in their animals. For example, swan breeders buy aquatic weed seeds screened by organic rice growers to ensure that ornamental characteristics are passed on.

It's easy when you're feeding an animal – it has no freedom of choice. We can't, however, coerce people to eat well. So, it is essential that we be persuaded to eat wholesome food, rather than junk food.

In 1936 The American Senate gave the following warning: "The alarming fact is that foods (fruits, vegetables and grains) now being raised on millions of acres of land that no longer contains enough of certain minerals are starving us – no matter how much of them we eat. No man of today can eat enough fruits and vegetables to supply his system with the minerals he requires for perfect health because his stomach isn't big enough to hold them". The 1930s saw the 'Dust Bowl' and the erosion of large parts of America's soil as the fertility of the prairies was finally used up. Agrichemical use kept the exhausted land in production but the missing minerals were never replaced, except on organic farms.

In August 2000 Kings College in London released the results of a research study: between 10 per cent and 30 per cent of adolescent girls have mild iron deficiency and those girls who were iron deficient had a significantly lower I.Q.

The Encyclopaedia of Natural Medicine
Michael Murray, Joseph Pizzorno
Little, Brown 1998
ISBN: 0 316 64678 4

Brain Food

think about it

"Jeeves is incredible in the brain-power department. He puts it down to the fact that he eats almost nothing but fish."
Bertie Wooster, P.G. Wodehouse

The healthy brain relies on a constant supply of essential nutrients – many of which come from the food we eat. Any interference, either in the growing or processing of food, that affects the nutritional make-up directly affects our body's ability to function properly. A few examples will show how important a balanced diet is to our general health.

Essential Fatty Acids
Oily fish such as herring, mackerel, sardines, salmon and tuna are rich sources of substances known as Essential Fatty Acids (EFAs), essential for effective food metabolism and for the regulation of cell growth and regeneration. Docosahexaenoic acid (DHA), for example, builds brain structure. Fifty per cent of the brain's DHA is formed while in the womb and the remainder in the first year of the baby's life.

So, Jeeves' legendary brain power owed as much to his mother's diet as it did to his own food choices. DHA is transmitted through the placenta and mother's milk, so the prenatal diet is vital. This period of brain growth is the baby's only chance to develop its full potential; it can't make up the deficit later in life. But eating fish later in life does help to maintain the brain.

EFAs are crucial for brain function, good vision, memory and learning. Research has shown that fish oil supplements help children with dyslexia, hyperactivity and even autism. In older people senile dementia and schizophrenia are linked to diets low in DHA.

Taking fish oil as a supplement is a quick fix

rather than a solution for DHA deficiency, though – and one that we may need to be wary of over time. Fish oil comes from the same sources that produce feed for intensive poultry, pig and salmon farms. It also comes with all the risks of pollutants that accumulate in fish, such as dioxins and PCBs.

Vegetarian parents need not worry. Non-fish eaters can still enjoy high DHA levels because healthy cells manufacture DHA from the 'omega-3' essential fatty acids found in vegetables. This function, however, is impaired by hydrogenated fat, frying oil, rancid oil, alcohol and excess cholesterol from animal products. It also is reduced by ageing, diabetes, low blood sugar and infections.

Omega-3 EFAs can be found in flax, hemp and pumpkin seeds, or their oils. Tofu, tempeh and dark green vegetables such as kale and parsley, as well as wheat grass and spirulina are also good sources. All chlorophyll cells in plants contain omega-3 so, cows that graze on grass have omega-3 in their meat and milk. Intensively reared cattle have high levels of saturated fat and little omega-3.

Iodine

The thyroid gland relies on the mineral iodine to produce its hormone, thyroxine, used to control metabolic rates, energy levels and brain development. The mental condition 'cretinism' was first diagnosed among Swiss children in mountain areas with no iodine content in the soil. In the 1930s 40 per cent of the people in Michigan had goitre, a symptom of iodine deficiency. Most of the world's iodine-deficient areas do not require the compulsory iodisation of salt (although Vietnam and India are beginning to iodise). Iodine readily washes out of soil so its best dietary source is from sea vegetables and fish – kelp tablets and sushi rolls for examples. And because iodine is not stored in the body, it must be consumed regularly to maintain healthy levels.

Antioxidants

'Free radicals' – reactive oxidant particles – damage the fatty brain-cell membranes making them susceptible to disease. Antioxidants help minimise free radical damage. Vitamins C, and E, and coenzyme Q10, betacarotene (from dark coloured fruits and vegetables including carrots and parsley) and flavonoids (including tea) act as antioxidants. Vitamin E is found in wholegrains but is not in refined flour products.

Blood sugar and oxygen

The levels of iron, glucose and oxygen in your blood make a big difference to brain function. Iron is a major component of haemoglobin in red blood cells, needed to carry oxygen around the body. High iron levels ensure high oxygen levels which, as long as there is enough glucose available for the process of metabolism, ensures that the brain can function at maximum capability. Taking a walk after a meal helps oxygenate the brain.

Amino acids

The neurotransmitters in the brain, that carry messages from one neuron cell to the next, are made from proteins, themselves made up of amino acids. Of the 20 naturally occurring amino acids, some are created in the body, others we have to gain from the food we eat. These are called 'essential' amino acids and can be gained from a balanced diet.

Of course, the brain responds to factors other than diet. Lead, in the air and in drinking water, should be avoided, as should stress and noise. Physical and mental exercise, relaxation and adequate sleep all help. In general, a diet rich in wholegrains and vegetables will provide nutrition for the brain, with oily fish providing a back-up supply when needed.

Brain Food
Lorraine Perretta
Hamlyn 2001
ISBN: 0 600 60335 0

Hydrogenation of Fat

butter wouldn't melt

Fats, perhaps because of the association with obesity, are sometimes seen as 'bad' food in the diet, to be avoided whenever possible. However, essential fatty acids (EFAs) are a vital part of a healthy diet and underpin the healthy functioning of the nervous system, not least foetal brain development. Yet we see the strange paradox in the USA where daily consumption of essential fatty acids is two to three times the required level, and still people suffer from heart disease, cancer and skin disease – diseases that are directly associated with EFA deficiencies. Why is this? The answer lies with hydrogenated fats.

What is Hydrogenation?

Hydrogenated fat is made with soya or rapeseed oil that has been refined in a process that involves crushing the seeds in a hexane solvent. Like its related chemicals (methane, propane, octane and heptane), hexane is highly inflammable, even explosive, but it also separates the oil from the rest of the seed and is then recovered by evaporation, leaving pure and, it is hoped, solvent-free vegetable oil.

The resulting vegetable oil is mixed with nickel particles and heated to 200°C. The mixture is then held at this temperature for up to six hours while hydrogen gas is pumped through at high pressure. The hydrogen atoms penetrate the oil molecules and form 'trans fats', new and complex substances that don't exist in nature. The cooled fat is very hard and can be stored as plastic-like beads for use in the manufacture of many common foods including:

- Margarine – using hydrogenated fat enables a higher level of polyunsaturates, but only at the cost of having a high level of trans fats.
- Bread – hydrogenated fat enables the loaf to have a higher water and air content, giving the appearance of greater bulk.
- Crisps and snacks – deep fried foods have a

drier, less oily texture as the trans fats do not melt at room temperatures.

- Biscuits – hydrogenated fat gives a less oily feel.

Prof Walter Willett at Harvard University conducted a study of 67,000 nurses who kept dietary records for 12 years. The results were conclusive: hydrogenated fat consumption is directly related to increased rates of heart disease, cancer, obesity and skin disease. The authors wrote: "Our findings must add to the concern that the practice of partially hydrogenating vegetable oils may have reduced the anticipated benefits of substituting these oils for highly saturated fats, and instead contributed to the occurrence of coronary heart disease".

In 1994 the Committee on Medical Aspects of Food Policy recommended a reduction in the amounts of hydrogenated fats in the British diet. The Soil Association reacted immediately stating that no hydrogenated fat should ever be present in organic food. Meanwhile, hydrogenated fats still make up 30 percent of the average Briton's fat intake, with the highest proportion among the lowest income groups, who consume less olive oil or butter and more non-organic margarine.

Why is Hydrogenation harmful?

Trans fats are so hard that you can hold them in your hand all day and they won't melt. When we eat fats they are absorbed into the system by fat receptors. But when these receptors receive hydrogenated fats they aren't quite sure what to do with them and they hold on to them. Imagine a ticket office queue where the person at the front can't decide what ticket to buy. People further back will drift away hoping to get through elsewhere. The same happens with hydrogenated fats: they clog up the fat receptors and the EFAs can't get through and end up being lost. So a person whose diet includes plenty of EFAs can still suffer from EFA deficiency. One way around this is to consume directly the oils that EFAs are converted to – hemp oil, evening primrose oil, flax oil and fish oils, for example. Better still, avoid hydrogenated fat in the first place.

Health implications

It was Willett's report that first brought hydrogenated trans fats under scrutiny. Recent studies have further confirmed trans fats as a major dietary health hazard. When McDonald's switched from using beef tallow to hydrogenated fat in 1990, the trans-fat content of their french fries rose from five per cent of overall fat to 43 per cent. The Community Nutrition Institute (CNI) in Washington D.C. attacked McDonald's for this decision stating that incidents of heart disease, obesity and diabetes would rise as a result. Rodney Leonard of the CNI claimed that the 'killer fries' would:

- lead to involuntary obesity. Despite the same caloric intake and exercise levels, people who regularly eat hydrogenated fats weigh at least two kilograms more than infrequent users.

- reduce sperm count in males and raise frequency of deformed sperm

- if eaten by expectant mothers lead to lower weight babies since trans fats interfere in the synthesis of important regulators of the birth process called prostaglandins. Michel Odent, the French natural birth pioneer, links the low consumption of hydrogenated fat in Japan with the comparatively low level of Caesarian and induced deliveries.

The other names under which hydrogenated fat appears include, 'vegetable margarine', 'vegetable fat', 'vegetable shortening', 'hardened fat' and 'vegetable fats and oils.'

'Vegetable oil' is the only description that guarantees no hydrogenation. 'Partially hydrogenated oil' is actually the worst, as it contains the highest levels of trans fats. Vanaspati or 'vegetable ghee' has the highest level of trans fats of any commonly used shortening and is frequently found in Indian cooking.

Fats That Heal, Fats That Kill
Udo Erasmus
Alive Book 1993
ISBN: 0 920 47038 6

Microwaves

soaking up some rays

A pocket full of melted chocolate led to the discovery of microwaves. An engineer working with early magnetrons, the microwave generators that are used in radar, reached into his pocket for a chocolate bar, only to get his fingers covered in goo. By 1947 the first microwave oven, the Raytheon 'Radarange' appeared.

The real boost for microwaves came from a combination of the growth of fast food, suburbia and freezer ownership. Food that had home-cooked appeal could be made on assembly lines, frozen and then reheated quickly in fast-food restaurants. Busy mothers could recapture lost time by buying frozen food, and still present the family a choice of different meals, available in minutes. The traditional family dinner was the casualty. Parents and kids no longer got together at least once a day for a meal and a talk. Junior could run in the door, 'nuke' some burgers and fries and dash off to meet his friends with barely a word exchanged.

Boiling, roasting, baking and grilling all work by transferring heat from a source into the food. The molecules of the food itself don't change, they just get warmer. Microwaves work differently. Every food molecule has a positive and negative pole, just like a magnet. Microwave energy alternates between positive and negative polarity billions of times a second and the same oscillation is induced in the molecules of food, particularly water. This agitation, as the molecules spin back and forth, creates friction that warms up the food. It also deforms the molecular structure of the food. In genetic engineering, microwaves are used to weaken molecular structure to make it easier to insert new genes.

So is it safe to use microwave ovens?

One thing is for sure – if microwaves melt the chocolate bars in your pocket what they do to other parts of your body doesn't bear thinking about. By 1971 safety standards to restrict radiation from microwaves had been introduced to protect domestic users and workers in fast-food restaurants from the damaging effects of radiation. Microwave owners are advised to check for loose door hinges and most manufacturers offer specialist services to check that emission levels are safe. Few microwave owners, however, actually call on this service.

But what about the food itself?

When microwaved food comes out of the microwave it is still buzzing with wave energy. So it's a good idea to let it settle down before eating – it can be unexpectedly hot. (Care should always be taken if microwaving a baby's bottle.) Microwaving changes the structure of food and produces radiolytic by-products, new molecules that don't occur in nature. Concern about such changes has led to research and a report in *The Lancet* in 1989 referred to the conversion of trans amino acids into non-nutritious forms in baby formula. One amino acid, L-proline, was converted into a form that harms the nervous system and kidneys.

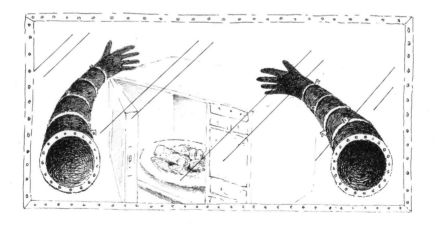

A Swiss clinical study found that people who had eaten microwaved food showed a decrease in the blood level of haemoglobin, which carries oxygen to the cells. White blood cell counts also decreased, reducing immune function. When this research was published in 1993 the Swiss electrical products dealers obtained a gagging order on the scientists who did the research. The scientists appealed to the European Court of Human Rights in 1998 and the gag was lifted.

In Russia, where microwaves have been banned since 1976, tests on food quality have found that microwaving formed carcinogens in meat, dairy products, fruit and vegetables and increased the cell-damaging and cancer-causing free radical content of root vegetables. Damage to the 'phytonutrients' in food, such as alkaloids, glucosides, galactosides and nitrilosides was also noted. We are still discovering the nutritional relevance of these 'secondary metabolites'.

Modern fan-assisted ovens are a better option. They don't emit radiation and they heat food almost as quickly as microwaves by using forced natural convection. At the same time the pleasures of cooking and of gathering for a meal with friends and family are being actively rediscovered, with the 'Slow Food' movement at the vanguard (See chapter 'Slow Food'). Microwaves do not play a role in this cultural renaissance.

Increased consumer awareness has encouraged restaurant owners to show when foods have been microwaved. As with information about genetic engineering, pesticide content and organic and regional origin, this knowledge empowers the consumer and almost always leads to higher food quality.

Vegetarians

the barmy army?

"It is my view that the vegetarian manner of living, by its purely physical effect on the human temperament, would most beneficially influence the lot of mankind."
Albert Einstein 1879-1955

Many of us will confess to thinking of vegetarians – let alone vegans – as slightly odd. But let us consider the situation.

In Great Britain 3,000 animals are killed for food – every minute. In the US nine million turkeys, chickens, pigs and cows are slaughtered every day. Meanwhile, major world religions such as Judaism, Islam, Christianity, Buddhism and Hinduism include vegetarianism among their core precepts.

Jews and Muslims get around the clear injunction to eschew the consumption of blood by draining the blood from the animal at the slaughterhouse. Buddhists in countries like Thailand employ Muslims to slaughter their meat, thereby absolving themselves of the act of killing.

Why, despite the repeated arguments from religious leaders, philosophers and health experts, do we still eat meat? The arguments for vegetarianism are convincing – morally, economically, environmentally and in terms of health.

Morally, there is the rule **"Thou shalt not kill"**. Most people recoil from killing animals. It is the dis-connection between liking animals and having to kill them to eat meat that persuades many people to become vegetarian. Since Pythagoras' time philosophers have linked a vegetarian lifestyle with peace, arguing that without a resistance to killing animals, the killing of fellow man becomes a question of degree rather than an absolute moral restraint. War becomes more likely, peace harder to sustain.

The combined weight of cattle on our planet exceeds that of human beings. To support this, one quarter of the earth's surface is used as livestock pasture. In the US three quarters of all grains and beans produced become animal feed. It takes seven kilos of maize and soybeans to produce a kilo of beef, three kilos to produce a kilo of chicken. Much of the destruction of the rain forests in Brazil has been to support soybean production for export to Europe for animal feed.

Ninety-five per cent of food poisoning cases are caused by animal products. The British Medical Association in 1998 announced: "The current state of food safety in the UK is such that all raw meat should be assumed to be contaminated with pathogenic organisms". The intensification of animal production means that animals ingest the faeces of fellow animals, increasing the risk of disease. So, in crowded conditions antibiotics are an essential ingredient of feed, yet inevitably in such conditions bacteria emerge which are antibiotic-resistant.

In 1983 E.coli O157:H7 was first diagnosed as a disease. Nobody is sure why the E.coli organism, most often found in minced meat, suddenly mutated into a more virulent, even fatal form. (Perhaps because of the location of the gene for virulence next to the gene for antibiotic resistance.) Two hundred Americans a year now die from E.coli and the second largest cause of kidney failure among American boys is E.coli infection. Heart disease and arthritis are linked to a meat-based diet, while bowel cancer is linked to beef consumption. The World Cancer Research Fund has shown that **vegetarians have lower overall mortality from, as well as lower risk of, heart disease, obesity and cancers.**

In Britain the Realeat Gallup poll puts vegetarianism at a steady five per cent of the adult population: seven per cent of women and three per cent of men describe themselves as

vegetarianism. The use of vast land and economic resources for the production of dairy products and eggs is also an issue, and a healthy vegan can claim higher absorption of nutrients and a lower intake of saturated fats.

Vegetarianism and veganism are growing rapidly now, after the UK's foot-and-mouth epidemic and other food scares. Perhaps the 'army' isn't so 'barmy' after all.

vegetarian, but among women aged 16-35 the number who avoid red meat is 25 per cent.

Vegans go a step further and avoid all dairy products and eggs. Dairy products depend on the lactation of female livestock following the birth of young. These calves, lambs and kids are slaughtered (particularly if male and therefore not future milk-producers) as they compete with humans for their mother's milk. Thus the concerns for animal welfare are not fully met by

> If it makes so much sense, why are vegetarians still a minority?

Mad Cowboy: Plain Truth From The Cattle Rancher Who Won't Eat Meat
Merzer, Lyman, Lyman
Scribner 2001
ISBN: 0 684 85446 5

Fasting

take a break

Most of us would be horrified at the thought of going for 30 years of our working life without a holiday, or even a weekend off. Some sacrifices are truly above and beyond the call of duty. Health, happiness and sanity depend on a break from the relentless routine. The brain needs a good night's sleep to recover from a day of thinking. Yet the digestive system works 24 hours a day for a lifetime without a chance to rest and recuperate.

The digestive systems of most people in the 'rich' world have never been empty from the moment of birth to the moment of death. There's always something in transit, always work to do.

The benefits of fasting have a long history in natural medicine and a far longer one in religion, where the spiritual benefits have an honourable tradition. We chafe at the restrictions and demands that society places upon us and long for freedom to do as we like. But we rarely chafe at the tyranny of the stomach, ever demanding, repeating its call on us to feed it several times a day. How could a complex and sophisticated creation such as a human being have become so abjectly dependent on a regular intake of food?

So, what happens if you don't eat? Quite a lot, and that's why for most generally healthy people it's such a good idea to fast occasionally.

There's no need to go off into the wilderness for 40 days and 40 nights. An 18-hour fast is a simple starter challenge. Eat dinner in the evening. Then don't eat until 2pm the following day. If that is manageable, try a 36-hour fast. Don't eat at all the following day, then 'break fast' on the morning of the next day.

Ultimately, the point of fasting is cleansing and rehabilitation. Just as you would drain the oil

from a car before adding new oil, so it is beneficial to let the body clear out accumulated wastes from time to time before eating again. It's inner spring cleaning. Fresh air, sunshine and exercise make it more effective.

What happens when you fast?
- The stomach gets a rest, returns to its normal size and rebuilds its hydrochloric acid level.
- The liver continues to regulate blood sugar level but it can also concentrate on getting rid of unwanted material.
- The pancreas, no longer dealing with unexpected intakes of sugars and no longer producing digestive enzymes, takes a well-earned break.
- The intestines recover their natural tone and the intestinal flora returns to optimal levels.
- Parasites diminish or die.

Most waste accumulates in the colon and it is here that distortion and loss of tone is greatest if we eat too much. The average Westerner carries five pounds of residues in the colon, mostly from low-fibre foods that have not made it through to excretion. Because this waste is usually absorbed back into the bloodstream, getting rid of it leads directly to feeling better, clearer skin, even clearer thoughts. Some people accelerate this cleansing with colonic irrigation – a very personal choice.

If you stop drinking tea or coffee during a fast after a day or two you will begin to experience caffeine withdrawal symptoms that include headaches and deep fatigue. These are the side effects of fasting and getting rid of toxins in the blood. It may be wise to drink small amounts of watery tea or coffee to minimise the impact of withdrawal – unless you intend to break caffeine addiction as a long-term goal.

Once you have fasted for short periods you will know how far you want to go. For a longer fast it may be best to begin with a 'semi-fast'. Rather than just water, have vegetable juices a few times a day. The seven-day brown rice diet of macrobiotics is another effective way; you learn to enjoy simple food and learn to chew.

With practice, fasting becomes much easier. Fasting with others reduces the sense of isolation and offers mutual support. There is a feeling of freedom and self-reliance that successfully completing a planned fast brings. Once you've done it you'll be hooked.

If you have weak kidneys, diabetes or any health problem that fasting might exacerbate, then seek professional advice before embarking on a fast.

Fasting-And Eating-For Health: A Medical Doctor's Program for Conquering Disease
Joel Fuhrman
St. Martin's Press (1998)
ISBN: 031218719X

Foreign Climes

positive approaches to agriculture

Different countries take different approaches to food and farming. Public-private partnerships in some countries have brought enormous benefits.

When Austria first applied for membership of the EU in the early 1990s, the 'first-come, first-served' principle of the Common Agricultural Policy (CAP) meant that Austrian farmers wouldn't get the same helpings from the gravy train as those of original member countries such as Germany, France and Italy. (As a late entrant to the EU, the UK pays £5 billion a year into the CAP and gets only half that amount back for British farmers). So the Austrian government decided to go for the niche market of organics and by the time Austria was a full member of the EU nine per cent of its farmland was organic. It produced so much organic maize and potatoes that it became a net exporter of maize for animal feed, corn syrup sweeteners, corn starch, corn grits for breakfast cereals and dried potato products.

Foresight and government policy ensured that both Austria's sensitive environment and anxious farmers have done well out of EU entry.

In 1990 in Schleswig-Holstein, the north German state that includes Hamburg and Kiel, the state government encouraged farmers to go organic. Because much of its land is at or below sea-level, the buildup of pesticides and other agricultural pollutants had become insupportable. But farmers expressed concern. They could sell organic vegetables and flax seeds, but what about the organic flax fibres? So the University of Kiel set up a commercial joint venture – Holstein Flachs – to develop organic linen fabrics for clothing and furnishing. Hugely successful, they

Organic land in Europe

2000/2001 figures
Percentage relates to
amount of agricultural
land given over to organic
production. In all cases the
figure is rising – in many
cases, with government
support, at a dramatic rate.

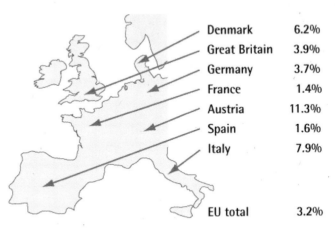

Denmark	6.2%
Great Britain	3.9%
Germany	3.7%
France	1.4%
Austria	11.3%
Spain	1.6%
Italy	7.9%
EU total	3.2%

now supply fabric to the burgeoning market for organic clothing. In 2001, buoyed by the project's success, Schleswig-Holstein announced plans to increase the area under organic cultivation.

In Denmark the government set targets for the organic production of animal feed, dairy and pork products. With government policy behind them, Danish producers invested in building organic capacity and the Danes now have the world's largest per capita consumption of organic food.

But it was in exports that Denmark had the real pay-off. When British supermarkets in the late 1990s were desperately seeking organic butter, milk and bacon to supply the exploding demand in the UK for organic food, the Danes were ready and willing to supply. The 'import gap' for organic food is a British national scandal, with 70 per cent of organic supplies imported, compared to less than 45 per cent for conventional food. Once imports are established it can be difficult for UK producers to recapture market share. Indeed, organic dairy farmers were faced with surpluses and low prices when UK production eventually caught up. Danish producers, meanwhile, enjoy strong sales in Scandinavia, Germany, Holland and even the US, supported by an efficient domestic market where 22 per cent of milk sold is organic, as well as 33 per cent of bread.

Italy has 2.5 million organic acres; 25 per cent of all organic land in the EU. Over 400 farms offer 'agri-bio' holidays where visitors can relax in organic countryside. Parental concern about BSE and GM food led the government in July 2000 actively to encourage the serving of organic food in school cafeterias, following the example set by the city of Ferrara. In 1994 Ferrara's kindergartens and nursery schools switched to serving organic pasta, bread, rice, beans and tomatoes and soon moved on to organic fruit and vegetables. By 1998 the programme was extended to all schools and now 80 per cent of school food is organic. Kids who eat organic as babies and eat organic at school tend to eat organic at home. Shops stock more organic food and prices fall as steady demand brings greater stability to the supply system. A 'virtuous circle' is in operation.

In Britain the 'best-value' principle of local authorities has meant price alone has been the criterion for purchasing decisions. Finally, in July 2002 this policy was modified to include environmental and health criteria, offering Britain's schools, hospitals and government canteens the chance to use organic food.

What took Britain so long? Well – Britain exports more agrichemicals than most. When the interests of parents and consumers clash with those of the British Agrochemicals Association, the Fertiliser Manufacturers Association and the British Pest Control Association it is difficult for civil servants to balance priorities. However, the cost to Britain's farmers, to the environment and to the balance of payments can be seen, with hindsight, to have been enormous – far greater than any savings to the agrichemical industry.

Regenerating Agriculture
Jules Pretty
Earthscan 1995
ISBN: 1 853 83198 0

Pick 'n' Mix

a little of what you fancy

An American military base was noted for its low level of sickness and high level of performance. When asked why, the base commander took the inquirer to the soldiers' mess, where a sergeant was seen standing at the front of the cafeteria line. From time to time he would send a soldier back to replenish his tray of food. "I count the colours," explained the sergeant. "As long as there are four different colours then the soldier eats."

Simplistic this may be, when set against the complexity of modern nutrition, but it has a long and honourable tradition. Cultures from as wide a range of countries as Italy, Lebanon, Scandinavia and Japan accept that it is better to set out a variety of choices than to prescribe a one-size-fits-all diet. In these countries, before the main course, each diner selects from a choice of starters. A healthy appetite will, given the selection, instinctively choose the right balance of foods. Antioxidants, anthyocyanins, phenolic compounds, fish oils, vitamin precursors, digestive aids, liver tonics and other valuable micronutrients are eaten before the diner moves on to the filling carbohydrate and protein part of the meal. In an age before vitamins and supplements, this was how people ensured good nutrition.

Antipasto is the Italian way: before the main dish the table is set with a range of bites – anchovies, tuna, olives, artichoke hearts, basil pastes, mushrooms, beans, grilled or raw chicory, celery hearts, fennel, carrots and broccoli. 'Bagna Cauda', a warm dipping sauce based on garlic, anchovies and olive oil is the perfect accompaniment to raw vegetable crudités.

In Lebanon 'mezze' does the same thing with a plate of raw vegetables such as radishes, carrots, cucumbers, mint sprigs, peppers, turnip, lettuce and tomatoes, along with parsley-rich tabouli salad, houmus, tahini, felafel and other pickles.

The 'smorgasbord' of Scandinavia sets out a variety of herring dishes, roasted and raw vegetables, grated beetroot or carrot salads, sweet and sour cabbage, all served with wholegrain pumpernickel bread or crispbreads.

Sushi in Japan ensures that the diner gets dietary essentials: digestion-enhancing miso soup, along with seaweed, oily fish, ginger pickle, tofu, daikon radish and umeboshi plums.

With so many different ingredients, 'leftover management' is the key to success. By pickling, marinating, grilling and serving cold, salting and other preservation methods, all the dishes can be rolled out every day, ensuring a continuous and varied selection of nutritional foods. After all, the healthiest diet mixes and balances all the food groups – carbohydrate, protein and fat.

Even the best ideas can be corrupted. The 'smorgasbord' concept can be abused. Tricon's 'Fast Food Smorgasbord' in the US aims to rival McDonald's, with multiple franchises – KFC, Taco Bell, Pizza Hut and Back Yard Burgers – all within one restaurant. Say goodbye to those family squabbles in the car over which fast food outlet

to visit. Now everyone can get their own favourite fatty, refined junk food under one roof.

Korean cuisine is considered by nutritionists to be the world's best. This is because it typically consists of about 70% carbohydrate, 17% protein and is very low in fat. By contrast, the typical Western diet is only about 40% carbohydrate and 15-20% fat, as well as 15-20% sugar.

Packaging

a necessary evil?

Banana skins, orange peels and wheat husks are natural packaging; all contain the edible inner part in transit and keep out bugs, dirt and other contaminants.

The earliest forms of 'added' packaging used natural materials – banana leaves, corn husks and gourds. All 100 per cent recyclable, they were discarded harmlessly when no longer needed. Willow baskets and terracotta urns were early man-made packaging that enabled the transport of solids and liquids over long distances without loss of quality. They could be reused until they were no longer useable.

Glass, paper and cardboard were the next wave of packaging materials and opened the way for branded, prepacked foods to feed the growing urban population. They were recyclable and, in the case of glass, reuseable. Old newspapers and printers' offcuts were used by fish and chip shops and grocers – and were used again to light fires, bed animals or insulate pipes. Things have come a long way since then.

In today's cash-rich, time-poor society, packaging has proliferated, creating mountains of waste in its wake. We are reaching a point with some ready-to-eat products where more energy is used in getting food to our lips than is represented by the food itself.

One sixth of our expenditure on food represents the cost of packaging, costing the average UK household £470 each year. Retailers innovate with new packaging that can help develop sub-brands and offer on-shelf excitement.

Britain produces 25 million tonnes of waste a year – 8 million tonnes are packaging. With collection, landfill and pollution clean-up costs all borne by the taxpayer, this represents a substantial indirect subsidy that masks the real cost of packaging to food processors. It distorts their judgement of how much packaging to use and whether it is recycled, or indeed, even recyclable.

There isn't enough landfill space to carry on like this. Something must be done. Fortunately, something is being done.

It is now widely agreed that all participants, from producer to end consumer, must share cradle-to-grave responsibility for the packaging that they produce and use. When producers are liable for material they introduce into the economy, they quickly find ways to minimise the amount they use, and to recycle the rest.

The EU aims, as a first step, to double the proportion of packaging that is recycled by 2007, setting a recycling target of between 55 and 70 per cent, up from the current minimum of between 25 and 45 per cent. The new rules will increase targets for recycling glass (60 per cent), paper and board (55 per cent), metals (50 per cent) and plastics (20 per cent).

Already, in Ireland, a plastic carrier bag carries a hefty premium on its cost that helps pay for cleaning up and recycling. This has led rapidly to increased durability and reusability of carrier bags and thus to a much higher rate of reuse. The UK is set to follow suit.

In 1982 Denmark prohibited aluminium cans and encouraged the use of glass containers that could be refilled and reused. Now they are opening the door to aluminium cans again, but with strict recycling conditions.

To produce aluminium, bauxite must be mined. Recycling 1 kg of aluminium saves 8 kg of bauxite, 4 kg of chemical products and 14 kilowatts of electricity. Aluminium can be recycled indefinitely, as reprocessing does not damage its structure. In 2000 the UK consumed five billion aluminium drinks cans, of which 42 per cent were recycled. This is a great improvement on the two per cent recycled in 1989, but is still much lower than Switzerland and Finland at 91 per cent. If all the aluminium cans used in the UK were recycled there would be 12 million fewer black binbags each year.

biodegradable and compostable trays for organic produce. Manufactured from potato starch and cellulose fibres from spruce (paper pulp waste) the 'Bio-pac' trays are freezable, ovenable and survive extreme temperature ranges (-40°C to + 220°C). The Bio-pac range will also include compostable films, netting, bags and absorbent pads for use with meat and fish. Such packaging offers a solution that covers all foods, organic or not – though the buying of food from local suppliers would, of course, massively reduce the huge energy costs of packaging still further.

When hidden subsidies for wasteful practices are eliminated and the true cost of packaging is paid by the users, innovative solutions to reduce, recycle and change the very nature of packaging emerge. All it takes is political will, and one may well wonder why it has all taken so long. But who knows, we may soon be able to buy fish and chips in old newspaper again – printed with lead-free inks, of course.

In Germany a group of leading organic food processors and wholesalers operate an 'Eight for All' scheme where all manufacturers agree to use a standard range of eight different glass jars and bottles. They can then cost-effectively accept returns and reuse each other's packaging.

Sainsbury's were confronted with the paradox that organic produce requires more packaging as regulations require that it be kept distinct from non-organic produce. The solution was to launch

Waste Watch
www.wastewatch.org.uk

Brave New World

guess what's coming to dinner

Why has genetic engineering been so controversial? Why is there such concern at the potential risks of eating foods that haven't been properly tested for safety? Most innovation by the food industry is demand-driven, a response to evolving consumer attitudes. Genetic engineering, however, came down from the top. It has been foisted on us. So, have the biotechnology corporations made a hideous mistake?

To answer the question we must look back to the early days of biotechnology, in the late 1980s.

With the discovery that it was possible to map genomes and manipulate genetic material the stock market went wild. Any company with a credible proposition was overwhelmed with funds as investors scrambled to be first aboard the gravy train. National governments committed hundreds of millions of public funds to support research. As with the dot.com boom, nobody could estimate future profits. but nobody wanted to miss out on the huge upside potential.

Biotechnology promised two main prizes:

A cure for cancer. Yet, by the late 1980s investors were losing faith in the ability of drug companies to find a cure for cancer. Biotechnology's proponents virtually guaranteed a breakthrough. Sadly, the search delivered nothing. British Biotech were UK leaders in the field of cancer research. Valued at £2bn in 1997, they dropped in value to £34 million by September 2002, a loss to investors of 98.3 per cent. Biotechnology companies can no longer raise funds on the stock market.

Control of the global market for food. Since time immemorial, people have tried to 'corner' the market in agricultural commodities. With the promise of genetically modified crops that would yield more, resist diseases, grow in depleted soils, taste better and stay fresh longer – money poured into companies like Monsanto.

The attempt to capture the food and farming markets fared poorly, except in the US. Here, Monsanto's attempt to dominate the agricultural sector is an example of corporate miscalculation on a colossal scale.

Monsanto's patent on their herbicide Roundup was due to expire by 2001. So they injected a Roundup-resistance gene into soybeans and corn and came up with Roundup Ready crops. Now fields could be sprayed year-round with Roundup without crops being affected. This ensured that farmers continued to pay a premium price for their herbicide. With money raised on Wall Street they bought up the leading seed companies in America, Canada, Argentina and India in order to force distribution of their new products. Launched in 1996, sales of GM seed boomed as farmers fell for a marketing pitch that promised higher yields and lower herbicide costs.

What have been the results of the GM experiment in North America?

1. Yields fell – Roundup Ready soybeans yield 6-11 per cent less than conventional varieties.

2. Herbicide use increased.

3. Gene Pollution. Farmers who didn't buy GM seeds found that cross-pollination had contaminated their crops anyway.

4. Litigation proliferated. Monsanto sent investigators into fields to snip leaf samples from crops. Their lawyers would then sue farmers who had traces of Monsanto's DNA growing in their fields. Some farmers hired their own analysts and proved that Monsanto's claims were groundless. (This led to a state law in North Dakota requiring that a state analyst must accompany seed company investigators). Most farmers, when faced with the threat of protracted legal action, meekly paid over $10,000 or so to Monsanto and signed a confidentiality agreement promising not to divulge the terms of the compromise.

5. Rogue herbicide-resistant oilseed rape plants emerged that were immune to three different herbicide groups. Farmers are forced to use more toxic older pesticides such as paraquat to get rid of them.

6. Contamination of non-GM crops undermined their value. The Starlink fiasco, in which an unapproved corn variety contaminated nearly half the American corn supply, cost the owners of

the seed, Aventis, $1bn paid out in compensation.

7. Export markets collapsed and prices fell. It is estimated that GM crops cost US farmers $12 billion between 1999 and 2001. There are nearly two million farmers in the US; in 2002 they will require subsidies of over 150 billion dollars, or $75000 per farmer.

8. Organic farmers suffered. In Saskatchewan farmers have given up growing organic oilseed rape because of contamination. The global market for GM seeds, for which no consumer demand exists, is $3.7 billion. The global market for organic food, for which real demand exists, is $20 billion.

9. Farmer groups across North American are united in opposition to the introduction of GM wheat, fearing even worse problems with an important export crop

10. Under pressure from consumers and farmers, legislation has been introduced into the US Congress to provide for GM labelling, to assign legal liability for the costs of GM disasters to the biotech companies and to protect farmers from legal harassment.

With such a negative outcome after only 6 years of GM crops, the rest of the world is understandably cautious.

In Argentina Monsanto met farmer resistance – so it abandoned the technology fees and sold farmers GM seeds on long term credit, with payment after harvest. In 2002 Argentine farmers could not pay their seed bills and Monsanto had to confiscate farmers' property. It wrote off $2 billion in the value of the seed companies and a $180 million in unpaid debts.

Brazil, which was set to go GM, decided to stay GM-free in order to tap into the lucrative market for non GM crops in the EU and Japan. In the EU,

China, India, Mexico, Sri Lanka, Canada, Thailand, Bosnia, Equador, Colombia, Guatemala, Nicaragua, Zambia, Zimbabwe, and Mozambique there has been dogged resistance to GM food imports and prolonged wrangling with US trade envoys. Farmers, used to saving seed, are reluctant to adopt a technology that prohibits (sic!) this practice and which has the 'Terminator' gene in reserve to enforce dependency on annual seed purchase. The US government is expending diplomatic capital in trying to force GM crops into export markets. Recipient nations reject GM food, even as food aid through the World Food Programme.

What future is there for GM crops? Nobody in Europe, Asia, Africa or Latin America wants to eat them. Few farmers want to grow them. Retailers are guaranteeing their products to be GM-free. No investor wants to invest in them. They may still have powerful political support, but the market is unlikely to change its verdict.

"Perhaps the biggest issue raised by these results is how to explain the rapid adoption of genetically engineered crops when farm financial impacts appear to be mixed or even negative." From 'The Adoption of Bio-engineered Crops' a US Department of Agriculture Report, May 2002.

"If anyone tells you that GM is going to feed the world, tell them that it is not. To feed the world takes political and financial will." Steve Smith, Director of biotech corporation Novartis (now Syngenta), in 2002.

"When you inject a supply-driven concept into a demand-driven market, it's a recipe for failure." Ron Olson, vice president of General Mills.

Lords of the Harvest
Daniel Charles
Perseus 2003
ISBN: 0 738 20773 X

Grow Your Own

when mud doesn't matter

*"Adopt the pace of nature, her
secret is patience"*
Emerson

When I return from my allotment with home-grown vegetables, I present them to the family and announce proudly: "Look at that, £40 worth of vegetables". To which a legitimate reply would be: "That would only cost £5 in the shops!"

So why bother? Even at the minimum wage, the cost in your time, horse manure, tools, seeds and seedlings far exceeds the cost of just buying your vegetables, washed and trimmed, from the supermarket. No slugs, no flea beetle, no white rot, no blight, no cabbage white butterfly, no backache. But that's only if you don't value the rewards of 'horticultural therapy'.

Growing food for your own table is richly satisfying – a healthful pursuit for mind, body and spirit. It can be done with the minimum of space in an urban flat or you can take on an allotment and get really serious.

A vegetable such as a beetroot or a cabbage, freshly harvested, lightly cooked or eaten raw, can easily be the central feature of a meal. In a restaurant you'd feel shortchanged, but at home, the vegetable grower's achievement brings pleasure to all who share it.

Growing your own food connects you with the elements of air, sunshine, earth and water. A tiny seed germinates, sends a tentative few leaves skyward and the gardener nurtures it until harvest. Watching this, learning patience yet being amazed at how rapidly some things can grow, brings a new level of respect for the power of plants. Passing time, the vagaries of weather, the changes of day-length as the seasons go through their cycle all root us in a deeper reality far from the artificial concerns of the 'real' world. Composting – the creating of soil from waste vegetable materials – is nature's alchemy. Converting base waste materials into pure horticultural gold is the Philosopher's Stone of gardening. The 'Rule of Return' is played out in slow motion as discarded vegetable parts, weeds and other 'rubbish' are transformed into crumbly brown compost that promises new fertility and life for the soil. When they move house, many people leave behind fixtures and fittings, but wouldn't dream of abandoning the compost heap. There is a real reward in working with the bacteria and fungi that add so much to the fertility of soil.

Growing your own food is good exercise, too. Like swimming, no part of the body is left unworked by hoeing, raking, digging, pulling weeds and planting seeds. Backache is a constant concern, but a respect for the back's limitations can ensure strengthening and toning without pain. An hour of gardening burns up 345 calories, half again as much as cycling. Bone health benefits both from activity and from exposure to sunlight. A different, deeper rhythm of nature takes over, to which our minds and bodies instinctively respond. It's mind work, too – plants are complex and challenging and learning to understand them is deeply stimulating.

Window boxes and indoor plants are nurseries for learning practical skills, even if you're only growing a tomato plant. But allotments are even better. Once the soil is in good condition the constant cycle of adding more compost is like a savings account – with a healthy interest rate repaid in tasty fresh vegetables. And there's a social life at allotments, too: mutual support, friendly advice, and the sharing of plants and surpluses.

Pick up a seed catalogue and read it alongside a newspaper. Which one fills you with hope?

You can have the fun of growing vegetables without an allotment or garden. WWOOF (Willing Workers on Organic Farms) enables you to help as a volunteer on organic farms in Britain and around the world.

Compost
Clare Foster
Cassell 2002
ISBN 0 304 36231 X

Education

grass-root concerns

How important food and nutrition are depends greatly on where you live and what you do.

The average American spends seven per cent of their income on food and non-alcoholic drink; the average Briton 10 per cent and the average Frenchman 15 per cent. Shopping, cooking and eating occupy one in six of our waking hours. So understanding the importance of food is one of the key 'life skills' we should all have acquired as children. Most food education is focused on food safety, avoiding food poisoning from bugs that shouldn't be in food in the first place.

In 12 years of primary and secondary education most children learn nothing about food, nutrition and health apart from tangential references in biology, where the human digestive system and metabolism are studied. Home economics, a study previously restricted to female students, has been abandoned altogether as a result of curriculum changes. Many students leave school able to calculate the collision time of two trains travelling at different speeds in opposite directions but unable to boil an egg, or bake a loaf of bread. There has been a marked decline in the number of students who opt to study food science or food technology.

In the four years of medical education that a doctor undergoes before qualification, just four hours are spent studying the subject of nutrition and health. In most hospitals the dietician or nutritionist is a lowly staff member, who is not allowed to diagnose and whose main role is to issue pre-programmed nutritional advice, mostly to diabetics. Hospital food is prepared with little attention to the individual's medical condition.

But children do get information about food. British children are exposed to 10 TV commercials an hour for confectionery and other sugary, fatty foods. Between the age of two and 12 a Canadian child will see 100,000 television commercials for food. At the age of three one in five American children are making specific brand-name requests for food. In the US Channel One's 12-minute in-classroom broadcast, featuring two minutes of commercials for every 10 minutes of news, is compulsory on 90 per cent of the school days in 80 per cent of the classrooms in 40 per cent of US middle and high schools. Companies pay up to $195,000 for a 30-second ad, knowing that they have a captive audience of 8 million students in 12,000 classrooms across the country. Coca-Cola pays schools and supplies educational material in exchange for exclusive rights to place drinks-vending machines in schools. They also lobby to allow students to have carbonated drinks in class.

How can children possibly obtain a balanced view of healthy nutrition in the face of such overwhelming corporate influence?

The Peckham Experiment from 1935-1939 showed that, when a group of families learned the fundamentals of nutrition and healthy eating their children did better at school, crime rates fell, domestic strife was reduced and overall

YES KIDS, IT'S TRUE, THERE REALLY IS MORE GOODNESS IN THE WRAPPER THAN IN THE BAR ITSELF!

health and social cohesion improved. The lessons learned have been applied infrequently since, but there are examples of change.

The Soil Association Demonstration Farms Network helps educate children in the origins of food. The aim is that every child in Britain will have visited an organic farm and been educated in the fundamentals of food production by the age of 12. Children remember 20 per cent of what they are told and 80 per cent of what they do, so farm visits have a real and lasting educational impact. Because organic farms usually have a mixture of crops and livestock the whole picture of food production can be studied. Demonstration farms allow kids to see animals close-up and helps them understand the connection between sustainable farming and care of the countryside. They can also buy fresh food from the farm shop, or taste something at the farm café. The challenge is then to encourage an ongoing interest in wholesome fresh food.

The Soil Association produces an education pack for primary school teachers. For secondary students, there are farm case studies with an accompanying video. Once they have an insight into the realities of farming and food production the students are more likely to reject a previously uncritical response to TV advertising and make independent judgements. They now know the full impact of their spending decisions.

These educated consumers form a bloc that food manufacturers ignore at their peril. In the words of a General Mills executive: "Our research shows that eight to nine per cent of American consumers will not buy a product if it contains GM ingredients – that's too large a chunk of our customer base to ignore unless GM offers some real benefits elsewhere". TV food advertising assumes ignorance among consumers. Brand loyalties cost a great deal to develop. Educated consumers will force a change in the values of companies that do not want to lose their expensively acquired customers.

In June 2002, the television company GMTV accepted a £1 million sponsorship deal with McDonald's for its cartoon slot on weekend mornings. Such a deal helps to target junk food at three to eight-year-old children. A child in that age range eating a McDonald's birthday party meal, choosing a cheeseburger, regular fries (with tomato ketchup), a regular coke and a slice of birthday cake would consume 889 kcalories: 81g of sugar; 27.7g of fat (11.5g saturated fat) and 1.6g of sodium (equivalent to 4g of salt). For a four to six-year-old this would be 60% of the maximum total recommended daily intake of saturated fat; 79% more sugar, and 128% more salt than the maximum total recommended daily intake. For a seven to ten-year-old it would be 53% of recommended daily intake of saturated fat; 58% more sugar and 33% more salt.

Stupid White Men ... and Other Sorry Excuses
for the State of the Nation!
Michael Moore
Penguin Books 2002
ISBN 0 141 01190 4

Some Conclusions

Dateline New York 2012 – The United Nations World Food and Health Organisation (WFHO) has published its State of the World Report.

Key data: The world's population has reached a plateau at 10 million. Life expectancy in all the world's nations continues to rise, with a global average of 80 years. Levels of heart disease, cancer, obesity and diabetes are in steep decline, ensuring a greatly improved quality of life for the aged. Infant and childhood mortality has plummeted. The ongoing programme of converting hospitals into luxury apartments continues, with 7,000 hospitals converted to other uses in the year 2011. The number of the world's citizens employed in agriculture continues to increase, as does the proportion of part-time agriculturalists. Farm sizes continue to reduce. Grain reserves now stand at 400 days. Starvation has gone the way of smallpox – totally eradicated. Land retirement continues as meat consumption worldwide falls to an annual average 6 kgs per person. GNP per person has risen with the reduction of military capacity, transferring investment into money-saving, planet-saving technologies. Emigration from Europe and North America continues to infuse Africa, Asia and Latin America with the capital and skills from returning immigrants. The world's economy continues to thrive since the Global Trade Justice Agreement of 2005 that led to the abolition of all US, EU and Japanese agricultural subsidies and protectionism following the Cairns Group Ultimatum of 2004. McDonald's recently announced that its sales of organic vegeburgers now outstrip beefburger sales by six to one, with wholewheat buns representing more than half of all buns sold. Monsanto, whose genomics seed division has continued to come up with naturally bred, landrace seed varieties tailored to the precise soil and climate requirements of the world's regions, announced record profits and commended the Small Farmers Seed Saving Programme for ensuring ideal genetic traits are maintained.

Fantasy? Not a bit of it. Nothing in this optimistic scenario should stretch the credulity of anyone who's read this little book. We have the technologies – in agriculture, preventive medicine, food processing and energy production – to avoid the immutable forces that lead us to starvation, obesity, disease and environmental degradation.

But here's the problem. We suffer a distorted food and agriculture system where powerful forces coerce and cajole governments to work against the public interests. Nobody really gains much from it. We didn't ask for the system we got – it has been sold as delivering the greatest goods, but in practice it demands ever-increasing subsidy and brings obesity, new more virulent bacterial diseases, increasing dependence on chemical fungicides, insecticides and herbicides as well as a cocktail of antibiotics, genetically engineered hormones, drugs and adulterants in our food and environment.

We need a new kind of accounting that counts all the costs, both in terms of shareholder profit and the rise in ill-health. Nowhere on the national account are the heartache of the bereaved, loss of earning power and agonising pain considered. If they were, we'd be in a very different situation with food.

Is cheap food worth the ill-health that is its concomitant? Is it worth the environmental destruction? The excessive use of fossil fuels? The risk of global warming and increasingly violent weather and flooding? Do we really want our children to enter puberty in hormonal turmoil, brought on by consumption of endocrine-disrupting chemicals in unpredictable interactions with the hormone imbalances inherent in obesity? The inevitable result in the longer run will be evolutionary degeneration. Surely this wasn't part of the deal?

But it's happened. Inexorable, focused pressure on governments around the world means the richest 20 per cent of the world's population suffer chronic obesity and food-related disease, and the poorest 20 per cent starve. The middle 60 per cent aren't doing that well, either – except, that is, for a rapidly growing minority who engage in 'joined-up thinking' about food, diet and farming. If you do the sums properly, i.e. from the perspective of society, eating unsubsidised, locally and organically grown wholesome food, free of artificial additives, is the answer for our own bodies – and ultimately, for our planet.

References

References: general

Visit our website at www.littleearth.co.uk/food for links to all web addresses mentioned here.

The Great Food Gamble, John Humphrys
Coronet 2002 ISBN: 0340770465
Food Nations,Warren Belasco, Philip Scranton
Routledge 2001 ISBN: 0415930774
Food Politics, Marion Nestle
University of California Press 2002 ISBN: 0520224655
Silent Spring, Rachel Carson
Penguin ISBN 0 141 18494 9
Living Planet Report 2002 World Wildlife Fund
www.panda.org

Useful websites

British Farm Standards: www.littleredtractor.org.uk
Centre for Alternative Technology: www.cat.org.uk
Corporate Watch: www.corporatewatch.org.uk
Department of the Environment, Food and Rural Affairs: www.defra.gov.uk
Earth Council: www.ecouncil.ac.cr
National Association of Farmer's Markets: www.farmersmarkets.net
Food and Agriculture Organization of the United Nations: www.fao.org
The Food Commission: http://ourworld.compuserve.com/homepages/foodcomm. They also produce a magazine.

Footprint: www.iclei.org
Forum for the Future: www.forumforthefuture.org.uk
Friends of the Earth: www.foe.co.uk
Organic Consumers Association: www.purefood.org
Organic Europe: www.organic-europe.net
Rachel's Environment and Health Weekly: www.rachel.org
Soil Association: www.soilassociation.org
Sustain: www.sustainweb.org
The Sustainable Society Directory: www.sustainable-society.co.uk
United State Department of Agriculture: www.fas.usda.gov
Waste Watch: www.wastewatch.org.uk
World Health Organisation: www.who.int
World Wildlife Fund: www.panda.org

References: Chapters

Pot Noodles and Civilisation • 'Obesity is changing human shape', BBC Online, 9 Sept 2002. News report from the British Association's science festival, Leicester.
Why Organics • The Worthington Study report. Source: 'Nutritional Quality of Organic Versus Conventional Fruits, Vegetables and Grains', by Virginia Worthington, M.S., Sc.D., C.N.S. published in *The Journal of Alternative and Complementary Medicine*, Vol. 7, No. 2, 2001 (pp. 161-173) • Research by Prof. Jules Pretty.'Food Security through Sustainable Agriculture'. Paper for Novartis Foundation for

Sustainable Development Symposium 'Nutrition and Development' Basel 30 Nov, 2000: www.foundation. novartis.com/symposium/jules_pretty.pdf • Compassion in World Farming. www.ciwf.co.uk. They are a leading international group, founded in 1967 as a reaction to the excesses of factory farming, that campaigns for improved standards of animal welfare in farming. • Soil degradation: 'Global Environment Outlook 3 – Past, Present and Future Perspectives'. United Nations Environment Programme, 2002. http://geo.unep-wcmc.org

Obesity • Obesity figures: 1999 estimate by the US Govt's Centers for Disease Control and Prevention, the body established to oversee America's health policy. www.cdc.gov/nccdphp/dnpa/obesity/defining.htm

Very Fast Food • UK food poisoning figures from Food Standards Agency Attitudes to Food Report 2001 • Obesity figures from WHO report 30 Oct 2002

Intensive Agriculture • Soil erosion: GEO3, UNEP, 2002. More details at: http://geo.unep-wcmc.org.

The (Not-so?) Green Revolution • Rise in number of hungry people: www.southcentre.org/publications/ occasional/paper04/paper4-04.htm. This refers to Rosset, Collins and Lappe 2000 'Lessons from the Green Revolution: Do We Need New Technology To End Hunger?' in *Tikkun Magazine* Vol 15, No 2 pp 52-56, March/April 2000. • Number of children dying from malnutrition refers to the UNICEF figure at: www.unicefusa.org/malnutrition/background.html • Useful figures at www.worldhunger.org/articles/ global/ray.htm#Table%201

Tastes Familiar • In August 1995 The Federation of American Societies for Experimental Biology (FASEB) presented to FDA the final report on its FDA-commissioned review of the safety of the food ingredients monosodium glutamate (MSG) and other free glutamates. On the basis of this report the FDA extended the requirement to label monosodium glutamate to requiring foods containing it, such as 'autolyzed yeast' or 'soy sauce' to add the phrase (contains glutamate), so that consumers could have some idea of how much glutamate they are consuming. http://vm.cfsan.fda.gov/~lrd/msg.txt

The ASA • The Willett Report: In 1980 Prof Walter Willett at the Harvard School of Public Health launched a study of 67,000 nurses who kept detailed dietary records over 12 years. He chose nurses because they are trained in accurate record-keeping. He then analysed their dietary patterns in the context of their health status. Much valuable nutritional information has come out of this ongoing study, in addition to establishing a significant link between hydrogenated fat consumption and a number of degenerative conditions. • Report: Willett, W. C. et al., 'Consumption of Trans-Fatty Acids in Relation to Risk of Coronary Heart Disease Among Women', Society for Epidemiology Research, Annual Meeting, June 1992, Abstract 249 53. Willett, W. C. et al., 'Intake of Trans Fatty Acids and Risk of Coronary Heart Disease Among Women', *Lancet* 341:581-585, 1993 54. www.heall.com/body/ healthupdates/food/hydrogenatedfat.html • An update report on hydrogenated fat and trans-fats available from www.hsph.harvard.edu/reviews/transfats.html • Sustain July 2001 report: From *TV Dinners - What's being served up by the advertisers?* ISBN: 1903060168 Order from www.sustainweb.org/pub_recent.asp

Sweet Nothings • Aspartame reported side effects including headaches, nausea, abdominal cramps, vision changes, diarrhoea and seizures. Full listings at: www.mac-archive.com/ns/side.html and www.321recipes.com/symptoms.html

The USA • www.nrcs.usda.gov/ has more information on the Natural Resources Inventory • www.greatplains.org/resource/nrisumm/savings.htm graphically illustrates that a 1 billion ton saving in soil erosion would be enough to fill a convoy, 250 trucks wide, of fully loaded dump trucks stretching nose to tail from New York to Los Angeles

Join the NFU • Bovine spongiform encephalopathy (BSE) is believed to be caused by a prion, or rogue protein, that leads to degeneration of brain cells and the creation of a sponge-like texture causing disorientation and death. • Simon Wetherall: NFU's Somerset chairman. Reported in the Western Daily Press 21st August, 2002 • Figures from 2001 Buckingham Research Association commissioned by founding members of *farm*. Launched on 4 Nov 2002, *farm* is 'a campaigning and membership organisation fighting for a viable future for independent and family farms. www.farm.org.uk.

Pesticides • The Pesticides Residues Committee was established to advise the Food Standards Agency and the Pesticides Safety Directorate on pesticides in food. They test 35-45 different foodstuffs each year, taking 4,000 samples, doing 90,000 individual tests at a Government-funded cost of £2 million. In Nov 2002 they recommended that fruit and vegetables – particularly potatoes – should be peeled before giving them to young children. • Organic farming permits the use of 'Bordeaux mixture' a copper sulphate compound used as a fungicide and 'rotenone' an extract of derris roots used for insect control. Before using these 'last resort' chemicals an organic farmer must justify such us to their certifying body and show what steps have been taken to prevent a recurrence of the problem that led to the need for chemical intervention.

Energy • Ethanol study: Professor David Pimentel, of the Cornell University College of Agriculture and Life Sciences. He chaired a US Dept of Energy panel that investigated the energetics, economics and environmental aspects of ethanol production. His article, 'Limits of Biomass Utilization', is in the *Encyclopedia of Physical Science and Technology*: 18 Volume Set Robert A. Meyers (Ed) Academic Press; ISBN: 0122269306

Organophosphates • 'Mad cow disease' theory: Mark Purdey is a Somerset farmer who refused to use organophosphate warble fly treatments on his cattle. They did not develop BSE. • His most recent article in *Science of Total Environment* 7 Oct 2002; 297(1-3):1-19 'Transmissible spongiform encephalopathies: a family of etiologically complex diseases – a review'. Bounias M, Purdey M. • Mark Purdey's website: www.purdeyenvironment.com • The 1997 Health and Safety Executive study was aimed specifically at assessing head lice treatments. • Monsanto's Roundup herbicide is an organophosphate, which would normally mean that it is an inhibitor to the enzyme cholinesterase and causes nerve system damage. However Monsanto claim that it is 'safe as table salt.' Action by the New York State Attorney General in 1997 required Monsanto to cease from describing Roundup as 'safe' or 'environmentally friendly.'

Oestrogen • Doctor Vyvyan Howard - Senior Lecturer In Foetal And Infant Toxicopathology At Liverpool University. *Endocrine Disrupters: Environmental Health and Policies* (Environmental Science and Technology

Library) Luc Hens (Editor), Vyvyan C. Howard (Editor), Polyxeni Nicolopoulou-Stamati (Editor). Kluwer Academic Publishers; ISBN: 0792370562 • Another interesting title to read *Our Stolen Future*, Theo Colborn, Abacus 1997 ISBN 0333901649

Genetically Modified Foods • Monsanto hived off by Pharmacia in Aug 2001, are one of the leading companies in genetic engineering and agriculture. Their main product is commodity crop seeds that have been engineered to be resistant to their Roundup herbicide. • Aventis, a Swiss pharmaceutical giant, have an agrochemical division which they are, at the time of writing, seeking to sell. Their products are resistant to Liberty, their proprietary herbicide brand.

Animal Welfare • 2012 animal rearing directives: The Council of Ministers agreed Directive 99/74/EC that will ban battery cages in 2012 but introduces phased implementation, beginning with an increase in the space allowance for caged birds taking effect from 1 Jan 2003. More details: www.defra.gov.uk/corporate/publications/pubcat/cvo/1999/chapter5.pdf • PETA (People for Ethical Treatment of Animals) campaigns against the abuse of animals in food production, entertainment and fashion. They seek the enforcement of animal welfare legislation which exists in the US and the UK but is implemented halfheartedly: www.peta.org.

Functional Foods • Nutritional needs: a survey by HealthFocus, an Atlanta, Georgia market research firm, showed that 3 out of 4 thought that their own nutritional needs are different from anyone else's. This makes the 'one size fits all' approach of functional food difficult to market on a wide scale. Functional food market report: www.healthfocus.net/function.htm

Antibiotics • Ionophore turkey poisoning: RSSL (Reading Scientific Services Laboratory) E-news Dec 2001. http://vmailw2k2.trinitevisp.co.uk:10018/food-e/011219.htm#article4 • Irradiation with Cobalt-60, also known as 'cold pasteurisation', involves placing highly radioactive Cobalt-60 (also used in cancer treatments) in a 'gun' directed at food. The gamma rays kill all bacteria in the food after a period of time. 'Radiolytic by-products', novel substances about which nothing is known, are created during irradiation and are the main cause for concern about the use of this technology as a way of dealing with pathogens in food.

Additives • The 1984 Food Labelling Regulations introduced E numbers into British food labelling. The 25% 'compound ingredient rule' is part of the same legislation. • E numbers come in categories, which are E100-180 = Colours; E200-252 = Preservatives; E260-297 = Acidities; E300-385 = Antioxidant; E400-429 = Thickeners; E430-499 = Emulsifiers; E620-640 = Flavour Enhancer; E950-967 = Sweeteners.

Wholegrains • Kuala Lumpur Lunatic Asylum: Fletcher, W 'Rice and beriberi: Preliminary report of an experiment conducted at the Kuala Lumpur Lunatic Asylum' *Lancet* 1907; i:1776-1779. It was found that patients who consumed brown rice experienced relief from the symptoms of beriberi, confirming that it was a nutritional deficiency disease. • Food pyramids: ideal - US Dept of Agriculture/US Dept of Health & Human Services. Actual - www.kde.state.ky.us/odff/nutrition

Nutrition and Food Quality • For 60 years, McCance and Widdowson's *The Composition of Foods* has been the authoritative source of information about the nutritional value of foods consumed in the UK. McCance and Widdowson's *The Composition of Foods*, Sixth summary edition. Cambridge: Royal Society of

Chemistry. Price: £45 ISBN 0-85404-428-0. • Document No. 264: was a Senate Report on Farmland Mineral Depletion. It looked at the consequences of the Dust Bowl and the decline in fertility of prairie soils. It also looked at the implications of this decline in fertility on food quality, particularly the mineral content of the American diet. • Iron deficiency report 2000: The connection made was that iron in blood, as haemoglobin, carries oxygen to the brain and the rest of the body. Without oxygen, the brain functions less efficiently as it cannot metabolise glucose (50% of the body's glucose consumption occurs in the brain). Other symptoms include general weakness, fatigue, brittle nails, paleness and loss of appetite.

Brain Food • Fish oil and dyslexia: Stordy, B. Jacqueline. 'Dark adaptation, motor skills, docosahexaenoic acid, and dyslexia' *American Journal of Clinical Nutrition*, Vol. 71 (suppl), January 2000, pp. 323S-26S • Details on fish oils and dyslexia are on the Dyslexia online magazine: www.dyslexia-parent.com/mag38.html • 'Free radicals': these are atoms or groups of atoms that have odd (unpaired) numbers of electrons. The free electrons cause them to react with other molecules in the body and if they react with DNA or cell membranes they can cause cell damage and cell death. Antioxidants such as beta-carotene and vitamins C and E interact with free radicals and neutralise them, preventing them from causing reactive damage to healthy cells.

Hydrogenation of Fat • In 1994, the Committee on Medical Aspects of Food and Nutrition Policy (COMA) published a report on Nutritional Aspects of Cardiovascular Disease. It recommended that no more than 35% of food energy intake should come from fat. Suggested proportions of fat in the diet:

Monounsaturated fatty acids -40%; Polyunsaturated fatty acids - 20%; Trans fatty acids - 6%; Saturated fatty acids - 34%

Microwaves • Microwave leakage testing: www.norwoodelectrical.co.uk/microwave-leakage-testing/index.htm • A microwave leakage detector is available from Cuthbertson Laird Group for £119. www.cuthbertsonlaird.co.uk/datasheets/martindale/tek500.html • Baby formula report: Lita Lee Ph.D reported in the 9 Dec, 1989 *Lancet*: • Microwaves and haemoglobin levels: report conducted by Swiss biologist Dr. H.U. Hertel in collaboration with Professor Bernard Blanc at the Swiss Federal Institute of Biochemistry of the University of Lausanne. They sought funding from the Swiss Government, which was refused on the grounds that the experiment would be a waste of time and unnecessary use of lab animals. They then performed a scaled-down study that identified the changes in blood quality. Blanc, B. H./Hertel, H. U. (1992): 'Comparative study about the influence on man by food prepared conventionally and in the microwave-over.' Raum & Zeit Special Nr.6, Ehlers, Sauerlach. More details at: www.vegan.swinternet.co.uk/articles/health/mw_danger.html • Russian microwave ban: research leading to the ban carried out at the Institute of Radio Technology at Klinsk, Byelorussia. Among effects of microwaving that led to a ban were: creation of d-Nitrodiethanolamine (a cancer-causing agent), creation of cancer-causing agents within dairy products and cereals, formation of free radicals in root vegetables, digestive and blood disorders in consumers of microwaved food, reduced nutritional content, destruction of nucleoproteins in meats. The 1976 ban was lifted by Gorbachev as part of Perestroika process.

Vegetarianism • Realeat, founded by Gregory Sams, were the manufacturers of the first VegeBurger™. The Realeat Survey is demographically representative, conducted at 200 sampling points across the UK. It has shown that vegetarianism has double from 2.1% of the population in 1984 to 5% in 1999. 45% of respondents said they were eating less meat. Details at: www.chaos-works.com/index2.html?/vegeburger6.html • Isaac Bashevis Singer: 1978 Nobel Laureate in Literature, Polish American author.

Fasting • More information at: www.healthy.net and www.freedomyou.com

Foreign climes • European organic land: provisional statistics, Sept 2002 from www.organic-europe.net

Pick 'n' Mix • Korean cuisine: *The Cambridge World History of Food*, Kenneth Kiple, Kriemhild Conee Omelas (Ed.) 2000 ISBN 0521402166

Packaging • Danish aluminium ban: The Danish government bowed to EU complaints in January 2002, announcing that the 20-year-old ban would end on condition that retailers charged a deposit of 1.50 Danish crowns (12p) to ensure customers returned empty cans.

Brave New World • 'Seeds of Doubt – North American Farmers' Experiences of GM Crops', Soil Association report Sept 2002 ISBN 0 905200 89 6 Summary and downloadable version available from: www.soilassociation.org

Grow Your Own • WWOOF PO Box 2675 Lewes BN7 1RB England, U.K. www.wwoof.org • Allotments: The 1887 Allotment Act required that local authorities fulfil all demand for allotments. Their popularity grew, particularly in wartime. From the 1950s to1990s many allotments fell into disuse and were taken over for housing development. Interest has since increased and allotment regeneration now attracts public and non-governmental funding. Water supply provision and secure fencing are key areas of investment that make allotments more attractive. For more information contact: The National Society of Allotment and Leisure Gardeners O Dell House, Hunters Road, Corby, Northants Tel: 01536 266576

Education • A schedule of 1999 percentage expenditure on food and non-alcoholic drinks in selected countries worldwide is at: www.ers.usda.gov/briefing/CPIFoodAndExpenditures/Data/table97.htm • The Peckham Experiment was established at the Pioneer Health Centre in one of the most deprived areas of London, under the supervision of Dr. Innes Pearce (a founding member of the Soil Association in 1946). Between 1935 and the outbreak of war in 1939, they worked with 1,206 families, comprising 3,911 individuals. Largely superseded by the introduction of the curative-based National Health Service, the prevention-oriented Peckham centre closed in 1950 due to lack of funds. In 1999 the introduction of £300 million budget Lottery-funded Healthy Living Centres (HLCs) in deprived areas marks a return the principles of the Peckham Experiment. HLC projects cover a range of activities including smoking cessation, dietary advice, physical activity, health screening programmes, training and skills schemes, arts programmes and complementary therapy. • Figures relating to MacDonald's birthday meal: The Food Commission, June 2002. • Dietary reference values, from which the Recommended Daily Allowance (RDA) for various food groups and substances are set, are established by the government's Committee on Medical Aspects of Food Policy (COMA)

Order More Books

The Little Food Book

The Little Food Book makes for a wonderfully stimulating read – one that hopefully changes your attitude to the food choices you make daily. To encourage you to bring your friends (and others) into this lively and urgent debate we are offering you the chance to order more copies of the book.

And don't forget our original title:

The Little Earth Book

Now in its third edition, this is as engrossing and provocative as ever, and continues to highlight the perilously fragile state of our planet. Little Earth makes the perfect companion to Little Food, so why not order a copy of each to make sure you understand just how much is at stake in our world today.

You can find out more about both these titles by visiting our website at **www.littleearth.co.uk**.

To order a copy of *The Little Food Book* or *The Little Earth Book*, (£6.99 each), send a cheque for the total amount, along with your name and address, to *Alastair Sawday Publishing* at:
ASP, The Home Farm, Barrow Gurney, Bristol BS48 3RW.
For credit card orders call **01275 464891** or order directly from our website.
Order 4 books and we'll send you an extra book **free**; just tell us how many of each book you would like. (This offer is not available via the web).

Travel Guides

Alastair Sawday also publishes the much-loved travel guide series – **Special Places to Stay.** If you are serious about travelling well – meeting interesting people, eating good regional food, avoiding chain hotels and burger-bars, etc – then you'd love these remarkable books. What's more, you'll probably also eat a lot of organic food and be 'pumping' your holiday money into the rural economy. Visit our website at **www.specialplacestostay.com**